State of the Union Speeches
By
Harry Truman

State of the Union Addresses

January 21, 1946

To the Congress of the United States:

A quarter century ago the Congress decided that it could no longer consider the financial programs of the various departments on a piecemeal basis. Instead it has called on the President to present a comprehensive Executive Budget. The Congress has shown its satisfaction with that method by extending the budget system and tightening its controls. The bigger and more complex the Federal Program, the more necessary it is for the Chief Executive to submit a single budget for action by the Congress.

At the same time, it is clear that the budgetary program and the general program of the Government are actually inseparable. The president bears the responsibility for recommending to the Congress a comprehensive set of proposals on all Government activities and their financing. In formulating policies, as in preparing budgetary estimates, the Nation and the Congress have the right to expect the President to adjust and coordinate the views of the various departments and agencies to form a unified program. And that program requires consideration in connection with the Budget, which is the annual work program of the Government.

Since our programs for this period which combines war liquidation with reconversion to a peacetime economy are inevitably large and numerous it is imperative that they be planned and executed with the utmost efficiency and the utmost economy. We have cut the war program to the maximum extent consistent with national security. We have held our peacetime programs to the level necessary to our national well-being and the attainment of our postwar objectives. Where increased programs have been recommended, the increases have been held as low as is consistent with these goals. I can assure the Congress of the necessity of these programs. I can further assure the Congress that the program as a whole is well within our capacity to finance it. All the programs I have recommended for action are included in the Budget figures.

For these reasons I have chosen to combine the customary Message on the State of the Union with the annual Budget Message, and to include in the Budget not only estimates for functions authorized by the Congress, but also for those which I recommend for its action.

I am also transmitting herewith the Fifth Quarterly Report of the Director of War Mobilization and Reconversion.[1] It is a comprehensive discussion of the present state of the reconversion program and of the immediate and long-range needs and recommendations.

[1] The report dated January 1, 1946, and entitled "Battle for Production" is printed in House Document 398 (79th Cong., 2d sess.).

This constitutes, then, as complete a report as I find it possible to prepare now. It constitutes a program of government in relation to the Nation's needs.

With the growing responsibility of modern government to foster economic expansion and to promote conditions that assure full and steady employment opportunities, it has become necessary to formulate and determine the Government program in the light of national economic conditions as a whole. In both the executive and the legislative branches we must make arrangements which will permit us to formulate the Government program in that light. Such an approach has become imperative if the American political and economic system is to succeed under the conditions of economic instability and uncertainty which we have to face. The Government needs to assure business, labor, and agriculture that Government policies will take due account of the requirements of a full employment economy. The lack of that assurance would, I believe, aggravate the economic instability.

With the passage of a full employment bill which I confidently anticipate for the very near future, the executive and legislative branches of government will be empowered to devote their best talents and resources in subsequent years to preparing and acting on such a program.

I. FROM WAR TO PEACE—THE YEAR

OF DECISION

In his last Message on the State of the Union, delivered one year ago, President Roosevelt said:

"This new year of 1945 can be the greatest year of

achievement in human history.

"1945 can see the final ending of the Nazi-Fascist reign of terror in Europe.

"1945 can see the closing in of the forces of retribution about the center of the malignant power of imperialistic Japan.

"Most important of all—1945 can and must see the substantial beginning of the organization of world peace."

All those hopes, and more, were fulfilled in the year 1945. It was the greatest year of achievement in human history. It saw the end of the Nazi-Fascist terror in Europe, and also the end of the malignant power of Japan. And it saw the substantial beginning of world organization for peace. These momentous events became realities because of the steadfast purpose of the United Nations and of the forces that fought for freedom under their flags. The plain fact is that civilization was saved in 1945 by the United Nations.

Our own part in this accomplishment was not the product of any single service. Those who fought on land, those who fought on the sea, and those who fought in the air deserve equal credit. They were supported by other millions in the armed forces who through no fault of their own could not go overseas and who rendered indispensable service in this country. They were supported by millions in all levels of government, including many volunteers, whose devoted public service furnished basic organization and leadership. They were also supported by the millions of Americans in private life—men and women in industry, in commerce, on the farms, and in all manner of activity on the home front—who contributed their brains and their brawn in arming, equipping, and feeding them. The country was brought through four years of peril by an effort that was truly national in character.

Everlasting tribute and gratitude will be paid by all Americans to those brave men who did not come back, who will never come back—the 330,000 who died that the Nation might live and progress. All Americans will also remain deeply conscious of the obligation owed to that larger number of soldiers, sailors, and marines who suffered wounds and sickness in their service. They may be certain that their sacrifice will never be forgotten or their needs neglected.

The beginning of the year 1946 finds the United States strong and deservedly confident. We have a record of enormous achievements as a democratic society in solving problems and meeting opportunities as they developed. We find ourselves possessed of immeasurable advantages—vast and varied natural resources; great plants, institutions, and other facilities; unsurpassed technological and managerial skills; an alert, resourceful, and able citizenry. We have in the United States Government rich resources in information, perspective, and facilities for doing whatever may be found necessary to do in giving support and form to the widespread and diversified efforts of all our people.

And for the immediate future the business prospects are generally so favorable that there is danger of such feverish and opportunistic activity that our grave postwar problems may be neglected. We need to act now with full regard for pitfalls; we need to act with foresight and balance. We should not be lulled by the immediate alluring prospects into forgetting the fundamental complexity of modern affairs, the catastrophe that can come in this complexity, or the values that can be wrested from it.

But the long-range difficulties we face should no more lead

to despair than our immediate business prospects should lead to the optimism which comes from the present short-range prospect. On the foundation of our victory we can build a lasting peace, with greater freedom and security for mankind in our country and throughout the world. We will more certainly do this if we are constantly aware of the fact that we face crucial issues and prepare now to meet them.

To achieve success will require both boldness in setting our sights and caution in steering our way on an uncharted course. But we have no luxury of choice. We must move ahead. No return to the past is possible.

Our Nation has always been a land of great opportunities for those people of the world who sought to become part of us. Now we have become a land of great responsibilities to all the people of all the world. We must squarely recognize and face the fact of those responsibilities. Advances in science, in communication, in transportation, have compressed the world into a community. The economic and political health of each member of the world community bears directly on the economic and political health of each other member.

The evolution of centuries has brought us to a new era in world history in which manifold relationships between nations must be formalized and developed in new and intricate ways.

The United Nations Organization now being established represents a minimum essential beginning. It must be developed rapidly and steadily. Its work must be amplified to fill in the whole pattern that has been outlined. Economic collaboration, for example, already charted, now must be carried on as carefully and as comprehensively as the political and security measures.

It is important that the nations come together as States in the Assembly and in the Security Council and in the other specialized assemblies and councils that have been and will be arranged. But this is not enough. Our ultimate security requires more than a process of consultation and compromise.

It requires that we begin now to develop the United Nations Organization as the representative of the world as one society. The United Nations Organization, if we have the will adequately to staff it and to make it work as it should, will provide a great voice to speak constantly and responsibly in terms of world collaboration and world well-being.

There are many new responsibilities for us as we enter into this new international era. The whole power and will and wisdom of our Government and of our people should be focused to contribute to and to influence international action. It is intricate, continuing business. Many concessions and adjustments will be required.

The spectacular progress of science in recent years makes these necessities more vivid and urgent. That progress has speeded internal development and has changed world relationships so fast that we must realize the fact of a new era. It is an era in which affairs have become complex and rich in promise. Delicate and intricate relationships, involving us all in countless ways, must be carefully considered.

On the domestic scene, as well as on the international scene, we must lay a new and better foundation for cooperation. We face a great peacetime venture; the challenging venture of a free enterprise economy making full and effective use of its rich resources and technical advances. This is a venture in which business, agriculture, and labor have vastly greater opportunities than heretofore. But they all also have vastly greater responsibilities. We will not measure up to those responsibilities by the simple return to "normalcy" that was tried after the last war.

The general objective, on the contrary, is to move forward to find the way in time of peace to the full utilization and development of our physical and human resources that were demonstrated so effectively in the war.

To accomplish this, it is not intended that the Federal Government should do things that can be done as well for the Nation by private enterprise, or by State and local governments. On the contrary, the war has demonstrated how effectively we can organize our productive system and develop the potential abilities of our people by aiding the efforts of private enterprise.

As we move toward one common objective there will be many and urgent problems to meet.

Industrial peace between management and labor will have to be achieved—through the process of collective bargaining—with Government assistance but not Government compulsion. This is a problem which is the concern not only of management, labor, and the Government, but also the concern of every one of us.

Private capital and private management are entitled to adequate reward for efficiency, but business must recognize that its reward results from the employment of the resources of the Nation. Business is a public trust and must adhere to national standards in the conduct of its affairs. These standards include as a minimum the establishment of fair wages and fair employment practices.

Labor also has its own new peacetime responsibilities. Under our collective bargaining system, which must become progressively more secure, labor attains increasing political as well as economic power, and this, as with all power, means increased responsibility.

The lives of millions of veterans and war workers will be greatly affected by the success or failure of our program of war liquidation and reconversion. Their transition to peacetime pursuits will be determined by our efforts to break the bottlenecks in key items of production, to make surplus property immediately available where it is needed, to maintain an effective national employment service, and many other reconversion policies. Our obligations to the people who won the war will not be paid if we fail to prevent inflation and to maintain employment opportunities.

While our peacetime prosperity will be based on the private enterprise the government can and must assist in many ways. It is the Government's responsibility to see that our economic system remains competitive, that new businesses have adequate opportunities, and that our national resources are restored and improved. Government must realize the effect of its operations on the whole economy. It is the responsibility of Government to gear its total program to the achievement of full production and full employment.

Our basic objective—toward which all others lead—is to improve the welfare of the American people. In addition to economic prosperity, this means that we use social security in the fullest sense of the word. And people must be protected from excessive want during old age, sickness, and unemployment. Opportunities for a good economy and adequate medical care must be readily available. Every family should build a decent home. The new economic rights to which I have referred on previous occasions is a charter of economic freedom which seeks to assure that all who will may work toward their own security and the general advancement; that we become a well-housed people, a well-nourished people, an educated people, a people socially and economically secure, an alert and responsible people.

These and other problems which may face us can be met by the cooperation of all of us in furthering a positive and well-balanced Government program—a program which will further national and international well-being.

II. THE FEDERAL PROGRAM

INTERNATIONAL AFFAIRS

I. FOREIGN POLICY

The year 1945 brought with it the final defeat of our enemies. There lies before us now the work of building a just and enduring peace.

Our most immediate task toward that end is to deprive our enemies completely and forever of their power to start another war. Of even greater importance to the preservation of international peace is the need to preserve the wartime agreement of the United Nations and to direct it into the ways of peace.

Long before our enemies surrendered, the foundations had been laid on which to continue this unity in the peace to come. The Atlantic meeting in 1941 and the conferences at Casablanca, Quebec, Moscow, Cairo, Tehran, and Dumbarton Oaks each added a stone to the structure.

Early in 1945, at Yalta, the three major powers broadened and solidified this base of understanding. There fundamental decisions were reached concerning the occupation and control of Germany. There also a formula was arrived at for the interim government of the areas in Europe which were rapidly being wrested from Nazi control. This formula was based on the policy of the United States that people be permitted to choose their own form of government by their own freely expressed choice without interference from any foreign source.

At Potsdam, in July 1945, Marshal Stalin, Prime Ministers Churchill and Attlee, and I met to exchange views primarily with respect to Germany. As a result, agreements were reached which outlined broadly the policy to be executed by the Allied Control Council. At Potsdam there was also established a Council of Foreign Ministers which convened for the first time in London in September. The Council is about to resume its primary assignment of drawing up treaties of peace with Italy, Rumania, Bulgaria, Hungary, and Finland.

In addition to these meetings, and, in accordance with the agreement at Yalta, the Foreign Ministers of Great Britain, the Soviet Union, and the United States conferred together in San Francisco last spring, in Potsdam in July, in London in September, and in Moscow in December. These meetings have been useful in promoting understanding and agreement among the three governments.

Simply to name all the international meetings and conferences is to suggest the size and complexity of the undertaking to prevent international war in which the United States has now enlisted for the duration of history.

It is encouraging to know that the common effort of the United Nations to learn to live together did not cease with the surrender of our enemies.

When difficulties arise among us, the United States does not propose to remove them by sacrificing its ideals or its vital interests. Neither do we propose, however, to ignore the ideals and vital interests of our friends.

Last February and March an Inter-American Conference on Problems of War and Peace was held in Mexico City. Among the many significant accomplishments of that Conference was an understanding that an attack by any country against any one of the sovereign American republics would be considered an act of aggression against all of them; and that if such an attack were made or threatened, the American republics would decide jointly, through consultations in which each republic has equal representation, what measures they would take for their mutual protection. This agreement stipulates that its execution shall be in full accord with the Charter of the United Nations Organization.

The first meeting of the General Assembly of the United Nations now in progress in London marks the real beginning of our bold adventure toward the preservation of world peace, to which is bound the dearest hope of men.

We have solemnly dedicated ourselves and all our will to the success of the United Nations Organization. For this reason we have sought to insure that in the peacemaking the smaller nations shall have a voice as well as the larger states. The agreement reached at Moscow last month preserves this opportunity in the making of peace with Italy, Rumania, Bulgaria, Hungary, and Finland. The United States intends to preserve it when the treaties with Germany and Japan are drawn.

It will be the continuing policy of the United States to use all its influence to foster, support, and develop the United Nations Organization in its purpose of preventing international war. If peace is to endure it must rest upon justice no less than upon power. The question is how justice among nations is best achieved. We know from day-to-day experience that the chance for a just solution is immeasurably increased when everyone directly interested is given a voice. That does not mean that each must enjoy an equal voice, but it does mean that each must be heard.

Last November, Prime Minister Attlee, Prime Minister MacKenzie King, and I announced our proposal that a commission be established within the framework of the United Nations to explore the problems of effective international control of atomic energy.

The Soviet Union, France, and China have joined us in the purpose of introducing in the General Assembly a resolution for the establishment of such a commission. Our earnest wish is that the work of this commission go forward carefully and thoroughly, but with the greatest dispatch. I have great hope for the development of mutually effective safeguards which will permit the fullest international control of this new atomic force.

I believe it possible that effective means can be developed through the United Nations Organization to prohibit, outlaw, and prevent the use of atomic energy for destructive purposes.

The power which the United States demonstrated during the war is the fact that underlies every phase of our relations with other countries. We cannot escape the responsibility which it thrusts upon us. What we think, plan, say, and do is of profound significance to the future of every corner of the world.

The great and dominant objective of United States foreign policy is to build and preserve a just peace. The peace we seek is not peace for twenty years. It is permanent peace. At a time when massive changes are occurring with lightning speed throughout the world, it is often difficult to perceive how this central objective is best served in one isolated complex situation or another. Despite this very real difficulty, there are certain basic propositions to which the United States adheres and to which we shall continue to adhere.

One proposition is that lasting peace requires genuine understanding and active cooperation among the most powerful nations. Another is that even the support of the strongest nations cannot guarantee a peace unless it is infused with the quality of justice for all nations.

On October 27, 1945, I made, in New York City, the following public statement of my understanding of the fundamental foreign policy of the United States. I believe that policy to be in accord with the opinion of the Congress and of the people of the United States. I believe that that policy carries out our fundamental objectives.

1. We seek no territorial expansion or selfish advantage. We have no plans for aggression against any other state, large or small. We have no objective which need clash with the peaceful aims of any other nation.

2. We believe in the eventual return of sovereign rights and self-government to all peoples who have been deprived of them by force.

3. We shall approve no territorial changes in any friendly part of the world unless they accord with the freely expressed wishes of the people concerned.

4. We believe that all peoples who are prepared for self-government should be permitted to choose their own form of government by their own freely expressed choice, without interference from any foreign source. That is true in Europe, in Asia, in Africa, as well as in the Western Hemisphere.

5. By the combined and cooperative action of our war allies, we shall help the defeated enemy states establish peaceful democratic governments of their own free choice. And we shall try to attain a world in which nazism, fascism, and military aggression cannot exist.

6. We shall refuse to recognize any government imposed upon any nation by the force of any foreign power. In some cases it may be impossible to prevent forceful imposition of such a government. But the United States will not recognize any such government.

7. We believe that all nations should have the freedom of the seas and equal rights to the navigation of boundary rivers and waterways and of rivers and waterways which pass through more than one country.

8. We believe that all states which are accepted in the society of nations should have access on equal terms to the trade and the raw materials of the world.

9. We believe that the sovereign states of the Western Hemisphere, without interference from outside the Western Hemisphere, must work together as good neighbors in the

solution of their common problems.

10. We believe that full economic collaboration between all nations, great and small, is essential to the improvement of living conditions all over the world, and to the establishment of freedom from fear and freedom from want.

11. We shall continue to strive to promote freedom of expression and freedom of religion throughout the peace-loving areas of the world.

12. We are convinced that the preservation of peace between nations requires a United Nations Organization composed of all the peace-loving nations of the world who are willing jointly to use force, if necessary, to insure peace.

That is our foreign policy.

We may not always fully succeed in our objectives. There may be instances where the attainment of those objectives is delayed. But we will not give our full sanction and approval to actions which fly in the face of these ideals.

The world has a great stake in the political and economic future of Germany. The Allied Control Council has now been in operation there for a substantial period of time. It has not met with unqualified success. The accommodation of varying views of four governments in the day-to-day civil administration of occupied territory is a challenging task. In my judgment, however, the Council has made encouraging progress in the face of most serious difficulties. It is my purpose at the earliest practicable date to transfer from military to civilian personnel the execution of United States participation in the government of occupied territory in Europe. We are determined that effective control shall be maintained in Germany until we are satisfied that the

German people have regained the right to a place of honor and respect.

On the other side of the world, a method of international cooperation has recently been agreed upon for the treatment of Japan. In this pattern of control, the United States, with the full approval of its partners, has retained primary authority and primary responsibility. It will continue to do so until the Japanese people, by their own freely expressed choice, choose their own form of government.

Our basic policy in the Far East is to encourage the development of a strong, independent, united, and democratic China. That has been the traditional policy of the United States.

At Moscow the United States, the Union of Soviet Socialist Republics, and Great Britain agreed to further this development by supporting the efforts of the national' government and nongovernmental Chinese political elements in bringing about cessation of civil strife and in broadening the basis of representation in the Government. That is the policy which General Marshall is so ably executing today.

It is the purpose of the Government of the United States to proceed as rapidly as is practicable toward the restoration of the sovereignty of Korea and the establishment of a democratic government by the free choice of the people of Korea.

At the threshold of every problem which confronts us today in international affairs is the appalling devastation, hunger, sickness, and pervasive human misery that mark so many areas of the world.

By joining and participating in the work of the United Nations Relief and Rehabilitation Administration the United States has directly recognized and assumed an obligation to give such relief assistance as is practicable to millions of innocent and helpless victims of the war. The Congress has earned the gratitude of the world by generous financial contributions to the United Nations Relief and Rehabilitation Administration.

We have taken the lead, modest though it is, in facilitating under our existing immigration quotas the admission to the United States of refugees and displaced persons from Europe.

We have joined with Great Britain in the organization of a commission to study the problem of Palestine. The Commission is already at work and its recommendations will be made at an early date.

The members of the United Nations have paid us the high compliment of choosing the United States as the site of the United Nations headquarters. We shall be host in spirit as well as in fact, for nowhere does there abide a fiercer determination that this peace shall live than in the hearts of the American people.

It is the hope of all Americans that in time future historians will speak not of World War I and World War II, but of the first and last world wars.

2. FOREIGN ECONOMIC POLICY

The foreign economic policy of the United States is designed to promote our own prosperity, and at the same time to aid in the restoration and expansion of world markets and to contribute thereby to world peace and world security.

We shall continue our efforts to provide relief from the devastation of war, to alleviate the sufferings of displaced persons, to assist in reconstruction and development, and to promote the expansion of world trade.

We have already joined the International Monetary Fund and the International Bank for Reconstruction and Development. We have expanded the Export-Import Bank and provided it with additional capital. The Congress has renewed the Trade Agreements Act which provides the necessary framework within which to negotiate a reduction of trade barriers on a reciprocal basis. It has given our support to the United Nations Relief and Rehabilitation Administration.

In accordance with the intentions of the Congress, lend-lease, except as to continuing military lend-lease in China, was terminated upon the surrender of Japan. The first of the lend-lease settlement agreements has been completed with the United Kingdom. Negotiations with other lend-lease countries are in progress. In negotiating these agreements, we intend to seek settlements which will not encumber world trade through war debts of a character that proved to be so detrimental to the stability of the world economy after the last war.

We have taken steps to dispose of the goods which on VJ-day were in the lend-lease pipe line to the various lend-lease countries and to allow them long-term credit for the purpose where necessary. We are also making arrangements under which those countries may use the lend-lease inventories in their possession and acquire surplus property abroad to assist in their economic rehabilitation and reconstruction. These goods will be accounted for at fair values.

The proposed loan to the United Kingdom, which I shall recommend to the Congress in a separate message, will contribute to easing the transition problem of one of our major partners in the war. It will enable the whole sterling area and other countries affiliated with it to resume trade on a multilateral basis. Extension of this credit will enable the United Kingdom to avoid discriminatory trade arrangements of the type which destroyed freedom of trade during the 1930's. I consider the progress toward multilateral trade which will be achieved by this agreement to be in itself sufficient warrant for the credit.

The view of this Government is that, in the longer run, our economic prosperity and the prosperity of the whole world are best served by the elimination of artificial barriers to international trade, whether in the form of unreasonable tariffs or tariff preferences or commercial quotas or embargoes or the restrictive practices of cartels.

The United States Government has issued proposals for the expansion of world trade and employment to which the Government of the United Kingdom has given its support on every important issue. These proposals are intended to form the basis for a trade and employment conference to be held in the middle of this year. If that conference is a success, I feel confident that the way will have been adequately prepared for an expanded and prosperous world trade.

We shall also continue negotiations looking to the full and equitable development of facilities for transportation and communications among nations.

The vast majority of the nations of the world have chosen to work together to achieve, on a cooperative basis, world security and world prosperity. The effort cannot succeed without full cooperation of the United States. To play our part, we must not only resolutely carry out the foreign policies we have adopted but also follow a domestic policy which will maintain full production and employment in the United States. A serious depression here can disrupt the whole fabric of the world economy.

3. OCCUPIED COUNTRIES

The major tasks of our Military Establishment in Europe following VE-day, and in the Pacific since the surrender of Japan, have been those of occupation and military government. In addition we have given much needed aid to the peoples of the liberated countries.

The end of the war in Europe found Germany in a chaotic condition. Organized government had ceased to exist, transportation systems had been wrecked, cities and industrial facilities had been bombed into ruins. In addition to the tasks of occupation we had to assume all of the functions of government. Great progress has been made in the repatriation of displaced persons and of prisoners of war. Of the total of 3,500,000 displaced persons found in the United States zone only 460,000 now remain.

The extensive complications involved by the requirement of dealing with three other governments engaged in occupation and with the governments of liberated countries require intensive work and energetic cooperation. The influx of some 2 million German refugees into our zone of occupation is a pressing problem, making exacting demands upon an already overstrained internal economy.

Improvements in the European economy during 1945 have made it possible for our military authorities to relinquish to the governments of all liberated areas, or to the United Nations Relief and Rehabilitation Administration, the responsibility for the provision of food and other civilian relief supplies. The Army's responsibilities in Europe extend now only to our zones of occupation in Germany and Austria and to two small areas in northern Italy.

By contrast with Germany, in Japan we have occupied a country still possessing an organized and operating governmental system. Although severely damaged, the Japanese industrial and transportation systems have been able to insure at least a survival existence for the population. The repatriation of Japanese military and civilian personnel from overseas is proceeding as rapidly as shipping and other means permit.

In order to insure that neither Germany nor Japan will again be in a position to wage aggressive warfare, the armament making potential of these countries is being dismantled and fundamental changes in their social and political structures are being effected. Democratic systems are being fostered to the end that the voice of the common man may be heard in the councils of his government.

For the first time in history the legal culpability of war makers is being determined. The trials now in progress in Nurnberg-and those soon to begin in Tokyo—bring before the bar of international justice those individuals who are charged with the responsibility for the sufferings of the past six years. We have high hope that this public portrayal of the guilt of these evildoers will bring wholesale and permanent revulsion on the part of the masses of our former enemies against war, militarism, aggression, and notions of race superiority.

4. DEMOBILIZATION OF OUR ARMED FORCES

The cessation of active campaigning does not mean that we

can completely disband our fighting forces. For their sake and for the sake of their loved ones at home, I wish that we could. But we still have the task of clinching the victories we have won—of making certain that Germany and Japan can never again wage aggressive warfare, that they will not again have the means to bring on another world war. The performance of that task requires that, together with our allies, we occupy the hostile areas, complete the disarmament of our enemies, and take the necessary measures to see to it that they do not rearm.

As quickly as possible, we are bringing about the reduction of our armed services to the size required for these tasks of occupation and disarmament. The Army and the Navy are following both length-of-service and point systems as far as possible in releasing men and women from the service. The points are based chiefly on length and character of service, and on the existence of dependents.

Over 5 million from the Army have already passed through the separation centers.

The Navy, including the Marine Corps and the Coast Guard, has discharged over one and a half million.

Of the 12 million men and women serving in the Army and Navy at the time of the surrender of Germany, one-half have already been released. The greater part of these had to be brought back to this country from distant parts of the world.

Of course there are cases of individual hardship in retention of personnel in the service. There will be in the future. No system of such size can operate to perfection. But the systems are rounded on fairness and justice, and they are working at full speed. We shall try to avoid mistakes, injustices, and hardship—as far as humanly possible.

We have already reached the point where shipping is no longer the bottleneck in the return of troops from the European theater. The governing factor now has become the requirement for troops in sufficient strength to carry out their missions.

In a few months the same situation will exist in the Pacific. By the end of June, 9 out of 10 who were serving in the armed forces on VE-day will have been released. Demobilization will continue thereafter, but at a slower rate, determined by our military responsibilities.

Our national safety and the security of the world will require substantial armed forces, particularly in overseas service. At the same time it is imperative that we relieve those who have already done their duty, and that we relieve them as fast as we can. To do that, the Army and the Navy are conducting recruiting drives with considerable success.

The Army has obtained nearly 400,000 volunteers in the past four months, and the Navy has obtained 80,000. Eighty percent of these volunteers for the regular service have come from those already with the colors. The Congress has made it possible to offer valuable inducements to those who are eligible for enlistment. Every effort will be made to enlist the required number of young men.

The War and Navy Departments now estimate that by a year from now we still will need a strength of about 2 million including officers, for the armed forces—Army, Navy, and Air. I have reviewed their estimates and believe that the safety of the Nation will require the maintenance of an armed strength of this size for the calendar year that is before us.

In case the campaign for volunteers does not produce that number, it will be necessary by additional legislation to extend the Selective Service Act beyond May 16, the date of expiration under existing law. That is the only way we can get the men and bring back our veterans. There is no other way. Action along this line should not be postponed beyond March, in order to avoid uncertainty and disruption.

DOMESTIC AFFAIRS

I. THE ECONOMIC OUTLOOK

Prophets of doom predicted that the United States could not escape a runaway inflation during the war and an economic collapse after the war. These predictions have not been borne out. On the contrary, the record of economic stabilization during the war and during the period of reconversion has been an outstanding accomplishment.

We know, however, that nothing is as dangerous as overconfidence, in war or in peace. We have had to fight hard to hold the line. We have made strenuous efforts to speed reconversion. But neither the danger of a postwar inflation nor of a subsequent collapse in production and employment is yet overcome. We must base our policies not on unreasoning optimism or pessimism but upon a candid recognition of our objectives and upon a careful analysis of foreseeable trends.

Any precise appraisal of the economic outlook at this time is particularly difficult. The period of demobilization and reconversion is fraught with uncertainties. There are also serious gaps in our statistical information. Certain tendencies are, however, fairly clear and recognition of them should serve as background for the consideration of next year's Federal Program. In general, the outlook for business is good, and it is likely to continue to be good—provided we control inflation and achieve peace in management labor relations.

Civilian production and employment can be expected to increase throughout the next year. This does not mean, however, that continuing full employment is assured. It is probable that demobilization of the armed forces will proceed faster than the increase in civilian employment opportunities. Even if substantial further withdrawals from the labor market occur, unemployment will increase temporarily. The extent to which this unemployment will persist depends largely on the speed of industrial expansion and the effectiveness of the policies of the Federal Government.

Along with extraordinary demand there are still at this time many critical shortages resulting from the war. These extraordinary demands and shortages may lead to a speculative boom, especially in the price of securities, real estate, and inventories.

Therefore, our chief worry still is inflation. While we control this inflationary pressure we must look forward to the time when this extraordinary demand will subside. It will be years before we catch up with the demand for housing. The extraordinary demand for other durable goods, for the replenishment of inventories, and for exports may be satisfied earlier. No backlog of demand can exist very long in the face of our tremendous productive capacity. We must expect again to face the problem of shrinking demand and consequent slackening in sales, production, and employment. This possibility of a deflationary spiral in the future will exist unless we now plan and adopt an effective full employment program.

2. GENERAL POLICIES—IMMEDIATE AND LONG-RANGE

During the war, production for civilian use was limited by war needs and available manpower. Economic stabilization required measures, to spread limited supplies equitably by rationing, price controls, increased taxes, savings bond campaigns, and credit controls. Now, with the surrender of our enemies, economic stabilization requires that policies be directed toward promoting an increase in supplies at low unit prices.

We must encourage the development of resources and enterprises in all parts of the country, particularly in underdeveloped areas. For example, the establishment of new peacetime industries in the Western States and in the South would, in my judgment, add to existing production and markets rather than merely bring about a shifting of production. I am asking the Secretaries of Agriculture, Commerce, and Labor to explore jointly methods for stimulating new industries, particularly in areas with surplus agricultural labor.

We must also aid small businessmen and particularly veterans who are competent to start their own businesses. The establishment and development of efficient small business ventures, I believe, will not take away from, but rather will add to, the total business of all enterprises.

Even with maximum encouragement of Production, we cannot hope to remove scarcities within a short time. The most serious deficiencies will persist in the fields of residential housing, building materials, and consumers' durable goods. The critical situation makes continued rent control, price control, and priorities, allocations, and inventory controls absolutely essential. Continued control of consumer credit will help to reduce the pressure on prices of durable goods and will also prolong the period during which the backlog demand will be effective.

While we are meeting these immediate needs we must look forward to a long-range program of security and increased standard of living.

The best protection of purchasing power is a policy of full production and full employment opportunities. Obviously, an employed worker is a better customer than an unemployed worker. There always will be, however, some frictional unemployment. In the present period of transition we must deal with such temporary unemployment as results from the fact that demobilization will proceed faster than reconversion or industrial expansion. Such temporary unemployment is probably unavoidable in a period of rapid change. The unemployed worker is a victim of conditions beyond his control. He should be enabled to maintain a reasonable standard of living for himself and his family.

The most serious difficulty in the path of reconversion and expansion is the establishment of a fair wage structure.

The ability of labor and management to work together, and the wage and price policies which they develop, are social and economic issues of first importance.

Both labor and management have a special interest. Labor's interest is very direct and personal because working conditions, wages, and prices affect the very life and happiness of the worker and his family.

Management has a no less direct interest because on management rests the responsibility for conducting a growing and prosperous business.

But management and labor have identical interests in the long run. Good wages mean good markets. Good business means more jobs and better wages. In this age of cooperation and in our highly organized economy the problems of one very soon become the problems of all.

Better human relationships are an urgent need to which organized labor and management should address themselves. No government policy can make men understand each other, agree, and get along unless they conduct themselves in a way to foster mutual respect and good will.

The Government can, however, help to develop machinery which, with the backing of public opinion, will assist labor and management to resolve their disagreements in a peaceful manner and reduce the number and duration of strikes.

All of us realize that productivity—increased output per man—is in the long run the basis of our standard of living. Management especially must realize that if labor is to work wholeheartedly for an increase in production, workers must be given a just share of increased output in higher wages.

Most industries and most companies have adequate leeway within which to grant substantial wage increases. These increases will have a direct effect in increasing consumer demand to the high levels needed. Substantial wage increases are good business for business because they assure a large market for their products; substantial wage increases are good business for labor because they increase labor's standard of living; substantial wage increases are good business for the country as a whole because capacity production means an active, healthy, friendly citizenry enjoying the benefits of democracy under our free enterprise system.

Labor and management in many industries have been operating successfully under the Government's wage-price policy. Upward revisions of wage scales have been made in thousands of establishments throughout the Nation since VJ-day. It is estimated that about 6 million workers, or more than 20 percent of all employees in nonagricultural and nongovernmental establishments, have received wage increases since August 18, 1945. The amounts of increases given by individual employers concentrate between 10 and 15 percent, but range from less than 5 percent to over 30 percent.

The United States Conciliation Service since VJ-day has settled over 3,000 disputes affecting over 1,300,000 workers without a strike threat and has assisted in settling about 1,300 disputes where strikes were threatened which involved about 500,000 workers. Only workers directly involved, and not those in related industries who might have been indirectly affected, are included in these estimates.

Many of these adjustments have occurred in key industries and would have seemed to us major crises if they had not been settled peaceably.

Within the framework of the wage-price policy there has been definite success, and it is to be expected that this success will continue in a vast majority of the cases arising in the months ahead.

However, everyone who realizes the extreme need for a swift and orderly reconversion must feel a deep concern about the number of major strikes now in progress. If long continued, these strikes could put a heavy brake on our program.

I have already made recommendations to the Congress as to the procedure best adapted to meeting the threat of work stoppages in Nation-wide industries without sacrificing the fundamental rights of labor to bargain collectively and ultimately to strike in support of their position.

If we manage our economy properly, the future will see us on a level of production half again as high as anything we have ever accomplished in peacetime. Business can in the future pay higher wages and sell for lower prices than ever before. This is not true now for all companies, nor will it ever be true for all, but for business generally it is true.

We are relying on all concerned to develop, through collective bargaining, wage structures that are fair to labor, allow for necessary business incentives, and conform with a policy designed to "hold the line" on prices.

Production and more production was the byword during the war and still is during the transition from war to peace. However, when deferred demand slackens, we shall once again face the deflationary dangers which beset this and other countries during the 1930's. Prosperity can be assured only by a high level of demand supported by high current income; it cannot be sustained by deferred needs and use of accumulated savings.

If we take the right steps in time we can certainly avoid the disastrous excesses of runaway booms and headlong depressions. We must not let a year or two of prosperity lull us into a false feeling of security and a repetition of the mistakes of the 1920's that culminated in the crash of 1929.

During the year ahead the Government will be called upon to act in many important fields of economic policy from taxation and foreign trade to social security and housing. In every case there will be alternatives. We must choose the alternatives which will best measure up to our need for maintaining production and employment in the future. We must never lose sight of our long-term objectives: the broadening of markets—the maintenance of steadily rising demand. This demand can come from only three sources: consumers, businesses, or government.

In this country the job of production and distribution is in the hands of businessmen, farmers, workers, and professional people-in the hands of our citizens. We want to keep it that way. However, it is the Government's responsibility to help business, labor, and farmers do their jobs.

There is no question in my mind that the Government, acting on behalf of all the people, must assume the ultimate responsibility for the economic health of the Nation. There is no other agency that can. No other organization has the scope or the authority, nor is any other agency accountable, to all the people. This does not mean that the Government has the sole responsibility, nor that it can do the job alone, nor that it can do the job directly.

All of the policies of the Federal Government must be geared to the objective of sustained full production and full employment-to raise consumer purchasing power and to encourage business investment. The programs we adopt this year and from now on will determine our ability to achieve our objectives. We must continue to pay particular attention to our fiscal, monetary, and tax policy, programs to aid business—especially small business—and transportation, labor-management relations and wage-price policy, social security and health, education, the farm program, public works, housing and resource development, and economic foreign policy.

For example, the kinds of tax measures we have at different times—whether we raise our revenue in a way to encourage consumer spending and business investment or to discourage it—have a vital bearing on this question. It is affected also by regulations on consumer credit and by the money market, which is strongly influenced by the rate of interest on Government securities. It is affected by almost every step we take.

In short, the way we handle the proper functions of government, the way we time the exercise of our traditional and legitimate governmental functions, has a vital bearing on the economic health of the Nation.

These policies are discussed in greater detail in the accompanying Fifth Quarterly Report of the Director of War Mobilization and Reconversion.

3. LEGISLATION HERETOFORE RECOMMENDED

AND STILL PENDING

To attain some of these objectives and to meet the other needs of the United States in the reconversion and postwar period, I have from time to time made various recommendations to the Congress.

In making these recommendations I have indicated the reasons why I deemed them essential for progress at home and abroad. A few—a very few—of these recommendations have been enacted into law by the Congress. Most of them have not. I here reiterate some of them, and discuss others later in this Message. I urge upon the Congress early consideration of them. Some are more urgent than others, but all are necessary.

(1) Legislation to authorize the President to create fact-finding boards for the prevention of stoppages of work in Nationwide industries after collective bargaining and conciliation and voluntary arbitration have failed—as recommended by me on December 3, 1945.

(2) Enactment of a satisfactory full employment bill such as the Senate bill now in conference between the Senate and the House—as recommended by me on September 6, 1945.

(3) Legislation to supplement the unemployment insurance benefits for unemployed workers now provided by the different States—as recommended by me on May 1945.

(4) Adoption of a permanent Fair Employment Practice Act—as recommended by me on September 6, 1945.

(5) Legislation substantially raising the amount of minimum wages now provided by law—as recommended by me on September 6, 1945.

(6) Legislation providing for a comprehensive program for scientific research—as recommended by me on September 6, 1945.

(7) Legislation enacting a health and medical care program—as recommended by me on November 19, 1945.

(8) Legislation adopting the program of universal training—as recommended by me on October 23, 1945.

(9) Legislation providing an adequate salary scale for all Government employees in all branches of the Government—as recommended by me on September 6, 1945.

(10) Legislation making provision for succession to the Presidency in the event of the death or incapacity or disqualification of the President and Vice President—as recommended by me on June 19, 1945.

(11) Legislation for the unification of the armed services—as recommended by me on December 19, 1945.

(12) Legislation for the domestic use and control of atomic energy—as recommended by me on October 3, 1945.

(13) Retention of the United States Employment Service in the Federal Government for a period at least up to June 30, 1947—as recommended by me on September 6, 1945.

(14) Legislation to increase unemployment allowances for veterans in line with increases for civilians—as recommended by me on September 6, 1945.

(15) Social security coverage for veterans for their period of military service—as recommended by me on September 6, 1945.

(16) Extension of crop insurance—as recommended by me on September 6, 1945.

(17) Legislation permitting the sale of ships by the Maritime Commission at home and abroad—as recommended by me on September 6, 1945. I further recommend that this legislation include adequate authority for chartering vessels both here and abroad.

(18) Legislation to take care of the stock piling of materials in which the United States is naturally deficient—as recommended by me on September 6, 1945.

(19) Enactment of Federal airport legislation-as recommended by me on September 6, 1945.

(20) Legislation repealing the Johnson Act on foreign loans—as recommended by me on September 6, 1945.

(21) Legislation for the development of the Great Lakes-St. Lawrence River Basin-as recommended by me on October 3, 1945.

4. POLICIES IN SPECIFIC FIELDS

(a) Extension of Price Control Act.

Today inflation is our greatest immediate domestic problem. So far the fight against inflation has been waged successfully. Since May 1943, following President Roosevelt's "hold the line" order and in the face of the greatest pressures which this country has ever seen, the cost of living index has risen only three percent. Wholesale prices in this same period have been held to an increase of two and one-half percent.

This record has been made possible by the vigorous efforts of the agencies responsible for this program. But their efforts would have been fruitless if they had not had the solid support of the great masses of our people. The Congress is to be congratulated for its role in providing the legislation under which this work has been carried out.

On VJ-day it was clear to all thinking people that the danger of inflation was by no means over. Many of us can remember vividly our disastrous experience following World War I. Then the very restricted wartime controls were lifted too quickly, and as a result prices and rents moved more rapidly upward. In the year and a half following the armistice, rents, food, and clothing shot to higher and still higher levels.

When the inevitable crash occurred less than two years after the end of the war, business bankruptcies were widespread. Profits were wiped out. Inventory losses amounted to billions of dollars. Farm income dropped by one-half. Factory pay rolls dropped 40 percent, and nearly one-fifth of all our industrial workers were walking the streets in search of jobs. This was a grim greeting, indeed, to offer our veterans who had just returned from overseas.

When I addressed the Congress in September, I emphasized that we must continue to hold the price line until the production of goods caught up with the tremendous demands. Since then we have seen demonstrated the strength of the inflationary pressures which we have to face.

Retail sales in the closing months of 1945 ran 12 percent above the previous peak for that season, which came in 1944. Prices throughout the entire economy have been pressing hard against the price ceilings. The prices of real estate, which cannot now be controlled under the law, are rising rapidly. Commercial rents are not included in the present price control law and, where they are not controlled by State law, have been increasing, causing difficulties to many businessmen.

It will be impossible to maintain a high purchasing power or an expanding production unless we can keep prices at levels which can be met by the vast majority of our people. Full production is the greatest weapon against inflation, but until we can produce enough goods to meet the threat of inflation the Government will have to exercise its wartime control over prices.

I am sure that the people of the United States are disturbed by the demands made by several business groups with regard to price and rent control.

I am particularly disturbed at the effect such thinking may have on production and employment. If manufacturers continue to hold back goods and decline to submit bids when invited—as I am informed some are doing—in anticipation of higher prices which would follow the end of price controls, we shall inevitably slow down production and create needless unemployment. On the other hand, there are the vast majority of American businessmen who are not holding back goods, but who need certainty about the Government pricing policy in order to fix their own long-range pricing policies.

Businessmen are entitled therefore to a dear statement of the policy of the Government on the subject. Tenants and housewives, farmers and workers—consumers in general—have an equal right.

We are all anxious to eliminate unnecessary controls just as rapidly as we can do so. The steps that we have already taken in many directions toward that end are a clear indication of our policy.

The present Price Control Act expires on June 30, 1946. If we expect to maintain a steady economy we shall have to maintain price and rent control for many months to -come. The inflationary pressures on prices and rents, with relatively few exceptions, are now at an all-time peak. Unless the Price Control Act is renewed there will be no limit to which our price levels would soar. Our country would face a national disaster.

We cannot wait to renew the act until immediately before it expires. Inflation results from psychological as well as economic conditions. The country has a clear right to know where the Congress stands on this all-important problem. Any uncertainty now as to whether the act will be extended gives rise to price speculation, to withholding of goods from the market in anticipation of rising prices, and to delays in achieving maximum production.

I do not doubt that the Congress will be beset by many groups who will urge that the legislation that I have proposed should either be eliminated or modified to the point where it is nearly useless. The Congress has a clear responsibility to meet this challenge with courage and determination. I have every confidence that it will do so.

I strongly urge that the Congress now resolve all doubts and as soon as possible adopt legislation continuing rent and price control in effect for a full year from June 30, 1946.

(b) Food subsidies.

If the price line is to be held, if our people are to be protected against the inflationary dangers which confront us, we must do more than extend the Price Control Act. In September we were hopeful that the inflationary pressures would by this time have begun to diminish. We were particularly hopeful on food. Indeed, it was estimated that food prices at retail would drop from 3 to 5 percent in the first six months following the end of the war.

In anticipation of this decline in food prices, it was our belief that food subsidies could be removed gradually during the winter and spring months, and eliminated almost completely by June 30 of this year. It was our feeling that the food subsidies could be dropped without an increase to the consumer in the present level of food prices or in the over-all cost of living.

As matters stand today, however, food prices are pressing hard against the ceilings. The expected decline in food prices has not occurred, nor is it likely to occur for many months to come. This brings me to the reluctant conclusion that food subsidies must be continued beyond June 30, 1946.

If we fail to take this necessary step, meat prices on July 1 will be from 3 to 5 cents higher than their average present levels; butter will be at least 12 cents a pound higher, in addition to the 5 cents a pound increase of last fall; milk will increase from 1 to 2 cents a quart; bread will increase about 1 cent a loaf; sugar will increase over 1 cent a pound; cheese, in addition to the increase of 4 cents now planned for the latter part of this month, will go up an additional 8 cents. In terms of percentages we may find the cost-of-living index for food increased by more than 8 percent, which in turn would result in more than a 3-percent increase in the cost of living.

If prices of food were allowed to increase by these amounts, I must make it clear to the Congress that, in my opinion, it would become extremely difficult for us to control the forces of inflation.

None of us likes subsidies. Our farmers, in particular, have always been opposed to them.

But I believe our farmers are as deeply conscious as any group in the land of the havoc which inflation can create. Certainly in the past eighteen months there has been no group which has fought any harder in support of the Government's price control program. I am confident that, if the facts are placed before them and if they see clearly the evils between which we are forced to choose, they will understand the reasons why subsidies must be continued.

The legislation continuing the use of food subsidies into the new fiscal year should be tied down specifically to certain standards. A very proper requirement, in my opinion, would be that subsidies be removed as soon as it is indicated that the cost of living will decline below the present levels.

(c) Extension of War Powers Act.

The Second War Powers Act has recently been extended by the Congress for six months instead of for a year. It will now expire, unless further extended, on June 30, 1946. This act is the basis for priority and inventory controls governing the use of scarce materials, as well as for other powers essential to orderly reconversion.

I think that this Administration has given adequate proof of the fact that it desires to eliminate wartime controls as quickly and as expeditiously as possible. However, we know that there will continue to be shortages of certain materials caused by the war even after June 30, 1946. It is important that businessmen know now that materials in short supply are going to be controlled and distributed fairly as long as these war-born shortages continue.

I, therefore, urge the Congress soon to extend the Second War Powers Act. We cannot afford to wait until just before the act expires next June. To wait would cause the controls to break down in a short time, and would hamper our production and employment program.

(d) Small business and competition.

A rising birth rate for small business, and a favorable

environment for its growth, are not only economic necessities but also important practical demonstrations of opportunity in a democratic free society. A great many veterans and workers with new skills and experience will want to start in for themselves. The opportunity must be afforded them to do so. They are the small businessmen of the future.

Actually when we talk about small business we are talking about almost all of the Nation's individual businesses. Nine out of every ten concerns fall into this category, and 45 percent of all workers are employed by them. Between 30 and 40 percent of the total value of all business transactions are handled by small business.

It is obvious national policy to foster the sound development of small business. It helps to maintain high levels of employment and national income and consumption of the goods and services that the Nation can produce. It encourages the competition that keeps our free enterprise economy vigorous and expanding. Small business, because of its flexibility, assists in the rapid exploitation of scientific and technological discoveries. Investment in small business can absorb a large volume of savings that might otherwise not be tapped.

The Government should encourage and is encouraging small-business initiative and originality to stimulate progress through competition.

During the war, the Smaller War Plants Corporation assisted small concerns to make a maximum contribution to victory. The work of the Smaller War Plants Corporation is being carried on in peacetime by the Federal Loan Agency and the Department of Commerce. The fundamental approach to the job of encouraging small concerns must be based on:

1. Arrangements for making private and public financial resources available on reasonable terms.

2. Provision of technical advice and assistance to business as a whole on production, research, and management problems. This will help equalize competitive relationships between large and small companies, for many of the small companies cannot afford expensive technical research, accounting, and tax advice.

3. Elimination of trade practices and agreements which reduce competition and discriminate against new or small enterprises.

We speak a great deal about the free enterprise economy of our country. It is competition that keeps it free. It is competition that keeps it growing and developing. The truth is that we need far more competition in the future than we have had in the immediate past.

By strangling competition, monopolistic activity prevents or deters investment in new or expanded production facilities. This lessens the opportunity for employment and chokes off new outlets for idle savings. Monopoly maintains prices at artificially high levels and reduces consumption which, with lower prices, would rise and support larger production and higher employment. Monopoly, not being subject to competitive pressure, is slow to take advantage of technical advances which would lower prices or improve quality. All three of these monopolistic activities very directly lower the standard of living—through higher prices and lower quality of product—which free competition would improve.

The Federal Government must protect legitimate business and consumers from predatory and monopolistic practices by the vigilant enforcement of regulatory legislation. The program will be designed to have a maximum impact upon monopolistic bottlenecks and unfair competitive practices hindering expansion in employment.

During the war, enforcement of antimonopoly laws was suspended in a number of fields. The Government must now take major steps not only to maintain enforcement of antitrust laws but to encourage new and competing enterprises in every way. The deferred demand of the war years and the large accumulations of liquid assets provide ample incentive for expansion. Equalizing of business opportunity, under full and free competition, must be a prime responsibility in the reconversion period and in the years that follow. Many leading businessmen have recognized the importance of such action both to themselves and to the economy as a whole.

But we must do more than break up trusts and monopolies after they have begun to strangle competition. We must take positive action to foster new, expanding enterprises. By legislation and by administration we must take specific steps to discourage the formation or the strengthening of competition-restricting business. We must have an over-all antimonopoly policy which can be applied by all agencies of the Government in exercising the functions assigned to them—a policy designed to encourage the formation and growth of new and freely competitive enterprises.

Among the many departments and agencies which have parts in the program affecting business and competition, the Department of Commerce has a particularly important role. That is why I have recommended a substantial increase in appropriations for the next fiscal year for this Department.

In its assistance to industry, the Department of Commerce

will concentrate its efforts on these primary objectives: Promotion of a large and well-balanced foreign trade; provision of improved technical assistance and management aids, especially for small enterprises; and strengthening of basic statistics on business operations, both by industries and by regions. To make new inventions and discoveries available more promptly to all businesses, small and large, the Department proposes to expand its own research activities, promote research by universities, improve Patent Office procedures, and develop a greatly expanded system of field offices readily accessible to the businesses they serve.

Many gaps exist in the private financial mechanism, especially in the provision of long-term funds for small- and medium sized enterprises. In the peacetime economy the Reconstruction Finance Corporation will take the leadership in assuring adequate financing for small enterprises which cannot secure funds from other sources. Most of the funds should and will be provided by private lenders; but the Reconstruction Finance Corporation will share any unusual risks through guarantees of private loans, with direct loans only when private capital is unwilling to participate on a reasonable basis.

(e) Minimum wage.

Full employment and full production may be achieved only by maintaining a level of consumer income far higher than that of the prewar period. A high level of consumer income will maintain the market for the output of our mills, farms, and factories, which we have demonstrated during the war years that we can produce. One of the basic steps which the Congress can take to establish a high level of consumer income is to amend the Fair Labor Standards Act to raise substandard wages to a decent minimum and to extend similar protection to additional workers who are not covered by the present act.

Substandard wages are bad for business and for the farmer. Substandard wages provide only a substandard market for the goods and services produced by American industry and agriculture.

At the present time the Fair Labor Standards Act prescribes a minimum wage of 40 cents an hour for those workers who are covered by the act. The present minimum wage represents an annual income of about $800 to those continuously employed for 50 weeks—clearly a wholly inadequate budget for an American family. I am in full accord with the proposal now pending in the Congress that the statutory minimum be raised immediately to 65 cents an hour, with further increases to 70 cents after one year and to 75 cents after two years. I also favor the proposal that the industry committee procedure be used to set rates higher than 65 cents per hour during the two-year interval before the 75-cent basic wage would otherwise become applicable.

The proposed minimum wage of 65 cents an hour would assure the worker an annual income of about $1,300 a year in steady employment. This amount is clearly a modest goal. After considering cost-of-living increases in recent years, it is little more than a 10-cent increase over the present legal minimum. In fact, if any large number of workers earn less than this amount, we will find it impossible to maintain the levels of purchasing power needed to sustain the stable prosperity which we desire. Raising the minimum to 75 cents an hour will provide the wage earner with an annual income of $1,500 if he is fully employed.

The proposed higher minimum wage levels are feasible without involving serious price adjustments or serious geographic dislocations.

Today about 20 percent of our manufacturing wage earners—or about 2 million-earn less than 65 cents an hour. Because wages in most industries have risen during the war, this is about the same as the proportion-17 percent—who were earning less than 40 cents an hour in 1941.

I also recommend that minimum wage protection be extended to several groups of workers not now covered. The need for a decent standard of living is by no means limited to those workers who happen to be covered by the act as it now stands. It is particularly vital at this period of readjustment in the national economy and readjustment in employment of labor to extend minimum wage protection as far as possible.

Lifting the basic minimum wage is necessary, it is justified as a matter of simple equity to workers, and it will prove not only feasible but also directly beneficial to the Nation's employers.

(f) Agricultural programs.

The farmers of America generally are entering the crop year of 1946 in better financial condition than ever before. Farm mortgage debt is the lowest in 30 years. Farmers' savings are the largest in history. Our agricultural plant is in much better condition than after World War I. Farm machinery and supplies are expected to be available in larger volume, and farm labor problems will be less acute.

The demand for farm products will continue strong during the next year or two because domestic purchases will be supplemented by a high level of exports and foreign relief shipments. It is currently estimated that from 7 to 10 percent of the total United States food supply may be exported in the calendar year 1946.

Farm prices are expected to remain at least at their present levels in the immediate future, and for at least the next 12 months they are expected to yield a net farm income double the 1935-39 average and higher than in any year prior to 1943.

We can look to the future of agriculture with greater confidence than in many a year in the past. Agriculture itself is moving confidently ahead, planning for another year of big production, taking definite and positive steps to lead the way toward an economy of abundance.

Agricultural production goals for 1946 call for somewhat greater acreage than actually was planted in 1945. Agriculture is prepared to demonstrate that it can make a peacetime contribution as great as its contribution toward the winning of the war.

In spite of supplying our armed forces and our allies during the war with a fifth to a fourth of our total food output, farmers were still able to provide our civilians with 8 percent more food per capita than the average for the five years preceding the war. Since the surrender of Japan, civilian food consumption has risen still further. By the end of 1945 the amount of the increase in food consumption was estimated to be as high as 15 percent over the prewar average. The record shows that the people of this country want and need more food and that they will buy more food if only they have the jobs and the purchasing power. The first essential therefore in providing fully for the welfare of agriculture is to maintain full employment and a high level of purchasing power throughout the Nation.

For the period immediately ahead we shall still have the

problem of supplying enough food. If we are to do our part in aiding the war-stricken and starving countries some of the food desires of our own people will not be completely satisfied, at least until these nations have had an opportunity to harvest another crop. During the next few months the need for food in the world will be more serious than at any time during the war. And, despite the large shipments we have already made, and despite what we shall send, there remain great needs abroad.

Beyond the relief feeding period, there will still be substantial foreign outlets for our farm commodities. The chief dependence of the farmer, however, as always, must be upon the buying power of our own people.

The first obligation of the Government to agriculture for the reconversion period is to make good on its price-support commitments. This we intend to do, with realistic consideration for the sound patterns of production that will contribute most to the long-time welfare of agriculture and the whole Nation. The period during which prices are supported will provide an opportunity for farmers individually to strengthen their position in changing over from a wartime to a peacetime basis of production. It will provide an opportunity for the Congress to review the needs of agriculture and make changes in national legislation where experience has shown changes to be needed. In this connection, the Congress will wish to consider legislation to take the place of the 1937 Sugar Act which expires at the end of this year. During this period we must do a thorough job of basic planning to the end that agriculture shall be able to contribute its full share toward a healthy national economy.

Our long-range agricultural policies should have two main objectives: First, to assure the people on the farms a fair share of the national income; and, second, to encourage an agricultural production pattern that is best fitted to the Nation's needs. To accomplish this second objective we shall have to take into consideration changes that have taken place and will continue to take place in the production of farm commodities—changes that affect costs and efficiency and volume.

What we seek ultimately is a high level of food production and consumption that will provide good nutrition for everyone. This cannot be accomplished by agriculture alone. We can be certain of our capacity to produce food, but we have often failed to distribute it as well as we should and to see that our people can afford to buy it. The way to get good nutrition for the whole Nation is to provide employment opportunities and purchasing power for all groups that will enable them to buy full diets at market prices.

Wherever purchasing power fails to reach this level we should see that they have some means of getting adequate food at prices in line with their ability to buy. Therefore, we should have available supplementary programs that will enable all our people to have enough of the right kind of food.

For example, one of the best possible contributions toward building a stronger, healthier Nation would be a permanent school-lunch program on a scale adequate to assure every school child a good lunch at noon. The Congress, of course, has recognized this need for a continuing school-lunch program and legislation to that effect has been introduced and hearings held. The plan contemplates the attainment of this objective with a minimum of Federal expenditures. I hope that the legislation will be enacted in time for a permanent program to start with the beginning of the school year next fall.

We have the technical knowledge and the productive capacity to provide plenty of good food for every man, woman, and child in the United States. It is time we made that possibility a reality.

(g) Resource development.

The strength of our Nation and the welfare of the people rest upon the natural resources of the country. We have learned that proper conservation of our lands, including our forests and minerals, and wise management of our waters will add immensely to our national wealth.

The first step in the Government's conservation program must be to find out just what are our basic resources, and how they should be used. We need to take, as soon as possible, an inventory of the lands, the minerals, and the forests of the Nation.

During the war it was necessary to curtail some of our long-range plans for development of our natural resources, and to emphasize programs vital to the prosecution of the war. Work was suspended on a number of flood control and reclamation projects and on the development of our national forests and parks. This work must now be resumed, and new projects must be undertaken to provide essential services and to assist in the process of economic development.

The rivers of America offer a great opportunity to our generation in the management of the national wealth. By a wise use of Federal funds, most of which will be repaid into the Treasury, the scourge of floods and drought can be curbed, water can be brought to arid lands, navigation can be extended, and cheap power can be brought alike to the farms and to the industries of our land.

Through the use of the waters of the Columbia River, for example, we are creating a rich agricultural area as large as the State of Delaware. At the same time, we are producing power at Grand Coulee and at Bonneville which played a mighty part in winning the war and which will found a great peacetime industry in the Northwest. The Tennessee Valley Authority will resume its peacetime program of promoting full use of the resources of the Valley. We shall continue our plans for the development of the Missouri Valley, the Arkansas Valley, and the Central Valley of California.

The Congress has shown itself alive to the practical requirements for a beneficial use of our water resources by providing that preference in the sale of power be given to farmers' cooperatives and public agencies. The public power program thus authorized must continue to be made effective by building the necessary generating and transmission facilities to furnish the maximum of firm power needed at the wholesale markets, which are often distant from the dam sites.

These great developmental projects will open the frontiers of agriculture, industry, and commerce. The employment opportunities thus offered will also go far to ease the transition from war to peace.

(h) Public works.

During the war even urgently needed Federal, State, and local construction projects were deferred in order to release sources for war production. In resuming public works construction, it is desirable to proceed only at a moderate rate, since demand for private construction will be abnormally high for some time. Our public works program should be timed to reach its peak after demand for private construction has begun to taper off. Meanwhile, however, plans should be prepared if we are to act promptly when the present extraordinary private demand begins to run out.

The Congress made money available to Federal agencies for their public works planning in the fiscal year 1946. I strongly recommend that this policy be continued and extended in the fiscal year 1947.

State and local governments also have an essential role to play in a national public works program. In my message of September 6, 1945, I recommended that the Congress vote such grants to State and local governments as will insure that each level of government makes its proper contribution to a balanced public construction program. Specifically, the Federal Government should aid State and local governments in planning their own public works programs, in undertaking projects related to Federal programs of regional development, and in constructing such public works as are necessary to carry out the various policies of the Federal Government.

Early in 1945 the Congress made available advances to State and local governments for planning public works projects, and recently made additional provision to continue these advances through the fiscal year 1946. I believe that further appropriations will be needed for the same purpose for the fiscal year 1947.

The Congress has already made provision for highway programs. It is now considering legislation which would expand Federal grants and loans in several other fields, including construction of airports, hospital and health centers, housing, water pollution control facilities, and educational plant facilities. I hope that early action will be taken to authorize these Federal programs.

With respect to public works of strictly local importance, State and local governments should proceed without Federal assistance except in planning. This rule should be subject to review when and if the prospect of highly adverse general economic developments warrants it.

All loans and grants for public works should be planned and administered in such a way that they are brought into accord with the other elements of the Federal Program.

Our long-run objective is to achieve a program of direct Federal and Federally assisted public works which is planned in advance and synchronized with business conditions. In this way it can make its greatest contribution to general economic stability.

(i) National housing program.

Last September I stated in my message to the Congress that housing was high on the list of matters calling for decisive action.

Since then the housing shortage in countless communities, affecting millions of families, has magnified this call to action.

Today we face both an immediate emergency and a major postwar problem.

Since VJ-day the wartime housing shortage has been growing steadily worse and pressure on real estate values has increased. Returning veterans often cannot find a satisfactory place for their families to live, and many who buy have to pay exorbitant prices. Rapid demobilization inevitably means further overcrowding.

A realistic and practical attack on the emergency will require aggressive action by local governments, with Federal aid, to exploit all opportunities and to give the veterans as far as possible first chance at vacancies. It will require continuation of rent control in shortage areas as well as legislation to permit control of sales prices. It will require maximum conversion of temporary war units for veterans' housing and their transportation to communities with the most pressing needs; the Congress has already appropriated funds for this purpose.

The inflation in the price of housing is growing daily.

As a result of the housing shortage, it is inevitable that the present dangers of inflation in home values will continue unless the Congress takes action in the immediate future.

Legislation is now pending in the Congress which would provide for ceiling prices for old and new houses. The authority to fix such ceilings is essential. With such authority, our veterans and other prospective home owners would be protected against a skyrocketing of home prices. The country would be protected from the extension of the present inflation in home values which, if allowed to continue, will threaten not only the stabilization program but our opportunities for attaining a sustained high level of home construction.

Such measures are necessary stopgaps-but only stopgaps. This emergency action, taken alone, is good—but not enough. The housing shortage did not start with the war or with demobilization; it began years before that and has steadily accumulated. The speed with which the Congress establishes the foundation for a permanent, long-range housing program will determine how effectively we grasp the immense opportunity to achieve our goal of decent housing and to make housing a major instrument of continuing prosperity and full employment in the years ahead. It will determine whether we move forward to a stable and healthy housing enterprise and toward providing a decent home for every American family.

Production is the only fully effective answer. To get the wheels turning, I have appointed an emergency housing expediter. I have approved establishment of priorities designed to assure an ample share of scarce materials to builders of houses for which veterans will have preference. Additional price and wage adjustments will be made where necessary, and other steps will be taken to stimulate greater production of bottleneck items. I recommend consideration of every sound method for expansion in facilities for insurance of privately financed housing by the Federal Housing Administration and resumption of previously authorized low-rent public housing projects suspended during the war.

In order to meet as many demands of the emergency situation as possible, a program of emergency measures is now being formulated for action. These will include steps in addition to those already taken. As quickly as this program can be formulated, announcement will be made.

Last September I also outlined to the Congress the basic principles for the kind of decisive, permanent legislation necessary for a long-range housing program.

These principles place paramount the fact that housing construction and financing for the overwhelming majority of our citizens should be done by private enterprise. They contemplate also that we afford governmental encouragement to privately financed house construction for families of moderate income, through extension of the successful system of insurance of housing investment; that research be undertaken to develop better and cheaper methods of building homes; that communities be assisted in appraising their housing needs; that we commence a program of Federal aid, with fair local participation, to stimulate and promote the rebuilding and redevelopment of slums and blighted areas—with maximum use of private capital. It is equally essential that we use public funds to assist families of low income who could not otherwise enjoy adequate housing, and that we quicken our rate of progress in rural housing.

Legislation now under consideration by the Congress provides for a comprehensive attack jointly by private enterprise, State and local authorities, and the Federal Government. This legislation would make permanent the National Housing Agency and give it authority and funds for much needed technical and economic research. It would provide additional stimulus for privately financed housing construction. This stimulus consists of establishing a new system of yield insurance to encourage large-scale investment in rental housing and broadening the insuring powers of the Federal Housing Administration and the lending powers of the Federal savings and loan associations.

Where private industry cannot build, the Government must step in to do the job. The bill would encourage expansion in housing available for the lowest income groups by continuing to provide direct subsidies for low-rent housing and rural housing. It would facilitate land assembly for urban redevelopment by loans and contributions to local public agencies where the localities do their share.

Prompt enactment of permanent housing legislation along these lines will not interfere with the emergency action already under way. On the contrary, it would lift us out of a potentially perpetual state of housing emergency. It would offer the best hope and prospect to millions of veterans and other American families that the American system can offer more to them than temporary makeshifts.

I have said before that the people of the United States can be the best housed people in the world. I repeat that assertion, and I welcome the cooperation of the Congress in achieving that goal.

(j) Social security and health.

Our Social Security System has just celebrated its tenth anniversary. During the past decade this program has supported the welfare and morale of a large part of our people by removing some of the hazards and hardships of the aged, the unemployed, and widows and dependent children.

But, looking back over 10 years' experience and ahead to the future, we cannot fail to see defects and serious inadequacies in our system as it now exists. Benefits are in many cases inadequate; a great many persons are excluded from coverage; and provision has not been made for social insurance to cover the cost of medical care and the earnings lost by the sick and the disabled.

In the field of old-age security, there seems to be no adequate reason for excluding such groups as the self-employed, agricultural and domestic workers, and employees of nonprofit organizations. Since many of these groups earn wages too low to permit significant savings for old age, they are in special need of the assured income that can be provided by old-age insurance.

We must take urgent measures for the readjustment period

ahead. The Congress for some time has been considering legislation designed to supplement at Federal expense, during the immediate reconversion period, compensation payments to the unemployed. Again I urge the Congress to enact legislation liberalizing unemployment compensation benefits and extending the coverage. Providing for the sustained consumption by the unemployed persons and their families is more than a welfare policy; it is sound economic policy. A sustained high level of consumer purchases is a basic ingredient of a prosperous economy.

During the war, nearly 5 million men were rejected for military service because of physical or mental defects which in many cases might have been prevented or corrected. This is shocking evidence that large sections of the population are at substandard levels of health. The need for a program that will give everyone opportunity for medical care is obvious. Nor can there be any serious doubt of the Government's responsibility for helping in this human and social problem.

The comprehensive health program which I recommended on November 19, 1945, will require substantial additions to the Social Security System and, in conjunction with other changes that need to be made, will require further consideration of the financial basis for social security. The system of prepaid medical care which I have recommended is expected eventually to require amounts equivalent to 4 percent of earnings up to $3,600 a year, which is about the average of present expenditures by individuals for medical care. The pooling of medical costs, under a plan which permits each individual to make a free choice of doctor and hospital, would assure that individuals receive adequate treatment and hospitalization when they are faced with emergencies for which they cannot budget individually. In addition, I recommended insurance benefits to replace part of the earnings lost through temporary sickness and permanent disability.

Even without these proposed major additions, it would now be time to undertake a thorough reconsideration of our social security laws. The structure should be expanded and liberalized. Provision should be made for extending coverage credit to veterans for the period of their service in the armed forces. In the financial provisions we must reconcile the actuarial needs of social security, including health insurance, with the requirements of a revenue system that is designed to promote a high level of consumption and full employment.

(k) Education.

Although the major responsibility for financing education rests with the States, some assistance has long been given by the Federal Government. Further assistance is desirable and essential. There are many areas and some whole States where good schools cannot be provided without imposing an undue local tax burden on the citizens. It is essential to provide adequate elementary and secondary schools everywhere, and additional educational opportunities for large numbers of people beyond the secondary level. Accordingly, I repeat the proposal of last year's Budget Message that the Federal Government provide financial aid to assist the States in assuring more nearly equal opportunities for a good education. The proposed Federal grants for current educational expenditures should be made for the purpose of improving the educational system where improvement is most needed. They should not be used to replace existing non-Federal expenditures, or even to restore merely the situation which existed before the war.

In the future we expect incomes considerably higher than before the war. Higher incomes should make it possible for

State and local governments and for individuals to support higher and more nearly adequate expenditures for education. But inequality among the States will still remain, and Federal help will still be needed.

As a part of our total public works program, consideration should be given to the need for providing adequate buildings for schools and other educational institutions. In view of current arrears in the construction of educational facilities, I believe that legislation to authorize grants for educational facilities, to be matched by similar expenditures by State and local authorities, should receive the favorable consideration of the Congress.

The Federal Government has not sought, and will not seek, to dominate education in the States. It should continue its historic role of leadership and advice and, for the purpose of equalizing educational opportunity, it should extend further financial support to the cause of education in areas where this is desirable.

(l) Federal Government personnel.

The rapid reconversion of the Federal Government from war to peace is reflected in the demobilization of its civilian personnel. The number of these employees in continental United States has been reduced by more than 500,000 from the total of approximately 2,900,000 employed in the final months of the war. I expect that by next June we shall have made a further reduction of equal magnitude and that there will be continuing reductions during the next fiscal year. Of the special wartime agencies now remaining, only a few are expected to continue actively into the next fiscal year.

At the same time that we have curtailed the number of employees, we have shortened the workweek by one-sixth or more throughout the Government and have restored holidays. The process of readjustment has been complicated and costs have been increased by a heavy turn-over in the remaining personnel—particularly by the loss of some of our best administrators. Thousands of war veterans have been reinstated or newly employed in the civil service. Many civilians have been transferred from war agencies to their former peacetime agencies. Recruitment standards, which had to be relaxed during the war, are now being tightened.

The elimination last autumn of overtime work for nearly all Federal employees meant a sharp cut in their incomes. For salaried workers, the blow was softened but by no means offset by the increased rates of pay which had become effective July 1. Further adjustments to compensate for increased living costs are required. Moreover, we have long needed a general upward revision of Federal Government salary scales at all levels in all branches—legislative, judicial, and executive. Too many in Government have had to sacrifice too much in economic advantage to serve the Nation.

Adequate salaries will result in economies and improved efficiency in the conduct of Government business—gains that will far outweigh the immediate costs. I hope the Congress will expedite action on salary legislation for all Federal employees in all branches of the Government. The only exception I would make is in the case of workers whose pay rates are established by wage boards; a blanket adjustment would destroy the system by which their wages are kept alined with prevailing rates in particular localities. The wage boards should be sensitive now, as they were during the war, to changes in local prevailing wage rates and should make adjustments accordingly.

I hope also that the Congress may see fit to enact legislation for the adequate protection of the health and safety of Federal employees, for their coverage under a system of unemployment compensation, and for their return at Government expense to their homes after separation from wartime service.

(m) Territories, insular possessions, and the District of Columbia.

The major governments of the world face few problems as important and as perplexing as those relating to dependent peoples. This Government is committed to the democratic principle that it is for the dependent peoples themselves to decide what their status shall be. To this end I asked the Congress last October to provide a means by which the people of Puerto Rico might choose their form of government and ultimate status with respect to the United States. I urge, too, that the Congress promptly accede to the wishes of the people of Hawaii that the Territory be admitted to statehood in our Union, and that similar action be taken with respect to Alaska as soon as it is certain that this is the desire of the people of that great Territory. The people of the Virgin Islands should be given an increasing measure of self-government.

We have already determined that the Philippine Islands are to be independent on July 4, 1946. The ravages of war and enemy occupation, however, have placed a heavy responsibility upon the United States. I urge that the Congress complete, as promptly and as generously as may be possible, legislation which will aid economic rehabilitation for the Philippines. This will be not only a just acknowledgment of the loyalty of the people of the Philippines, but it will help to avoid the economic chaos which otherwise will be their heritage from our common war. Perhaps no event in the long centuries of colonialism gives more hope for the pattern of the future than the independence of the Philippines.

The District of Columbia, because of its special relation to the Federal Government, has been treated since 1800 as a dependent area. We should move toward a greater measure of local self-government consistent with the constitutional status of the District. We should take adequate steps to assure that citizens of the United States are not denied their franchise merely because they reside at the Nation's Capital.

III. THE BUDGET FOR THE FEDERAL PROGRAM

FOR THE FISCAL YEAR 1947

SUMMARY OF THE BUDGET

For the first time since the fiscal year 1930 the Budget for the next fiscal year will require no increase in the national debt.

Expenditures of all kinds, authorized and recommended, in the next year are estimated at just above 35.8 billion dollars. Net receipts are estimated at 31.5 billion dollars. The estimated difference of 4.3 billion dollars will be met by a reduction in the very substantial balance which will be in the Treasury during the next fiscal year.

A large part of the activities outside defense and war liquidation, aftermath of war, and international finance, classified as "other activities" in a following table, is still due to repercussions of the war. These "other activities" include more than 2 billion dollars for aids to agriculture and net outlays for the Commodity Credit Corporation-almost double the expenditures for the same purposes in prewar years. This increase is due mainly to expenditures for purposes of price stabilization and price support resulting from the war food production program. Other increases in this category are due to the fact that certain wartime agencies now in the process of liquidation are included in this group of activities. If all expenditures for those activities which are directly or indirectly related to the war are excluded, the residual expenditures are below those for corresponding activities in prewar years. In making this comparison account should be taken of the fact that, while prewar expenditures were affected by direct relief and work relief for the unemployed, the postwar budgets are affected by the considerable increase in pay rates and other increases in costs and prices.

To elaborate, the Budget, as I have remarked above, reflects on both sides of the ledger the Government's program as recommended by the Executive. It includes estimates not only of expenditures and receipts for which legislative authority already exists, but also of expenditures and receipts for which authorization is recommended.

The Budget total for the next fiscal year, the year that ends on June 30, 1947, is estimated at just above 35.8 billion dollars-about a third of the budgets for global war, although nearly four times the prewar budgets. This estimate is based on the assumption that a rapid liquidation of the war program will be associated with rapid reconversion and expansion of peacetime production. The total includes net outlays of Government corporations.

The estimated expenditures in the next and current fiscal year compare as follows with those of a year of global war and a prewar year:

Total Budget expenditures

Fiscal year: (in millions)

1947 $35, 860

1946 67,229

1945 100, 031

1940 9,252

Although allowances for occupation, demobilization, and defense are drastically reduced in the fiscal year 1947, they will still amount to 42 percent of the total Budget. The so-called "aftermath of war" expenditures account for a further 30 percent of the total. The total of all other programs, which was drastically cut during the war, is increasing again as liquidation of the war program proceeds and renewed emphasis is placed on the peacetime objectives of the Government.

On the other side of the ledger, net receipts are estimated at 31.5 billion dollars. This estimate assumes that all existing taxes will continue all through the fiscal year 1947. Included are the extraordinary receipts from the disposal of surplus property.

As a result, estimated expenditures will exceed estimated receipts by 4.3 billion dollars. This amount can be provided by a reduction in the cash balance in the Treasury. Thus, after a long period of increasing public debt resulting from depression budgets and war budgets, it is anticipated that no increase in the Federal debt will be required next year.

FEDERAL BUDGET EXPENDITURES AND BUDGET RECEIPTS

Including net outlays of Government corporations and credit agencies (based on existing and proposed legislation)

Fiscal year

Expenditures: 1946 1947

Defense, war, and war liquidation $49,000 $15,000

Aftermath of war: Veterans, interest, refunds 10,813 10,793

International finance (including proposed legislation) 2,614 2,754

Other activities 4,552 5,813

Activities based on proposed legislation

(excluding international finance) 2501,500

Total expenditures 67, 229 35, 860

Receipts (net) 38, 60931,513

Excess of expenditures 28,620 4,347

The current fiscal year, 1946, is a year of transition. When the year opened, in July 1945, we were still fighting a major war, and Federal expenditures were running at an annual rate of about 100 billion dollars. By June 1946 that rate will be more than cut in half. The Budget total for the current fiscal year is now estimated at 67.2 billion dollars, of which more than two-thirds provides for war and war liquidation. Since net receipts are estimated at 38.6 billion dollars, there will be an excess of expenditures of 28.6 billion dollars for the current fiscal year.

For all programs discussed in this Message I estimate the total of Budget appropriations and authorizations (including reappropriations and permanent appropriations) at 30,982 million dollars for the fiscal year 1947. Of this amount, present permanent appropriations are expected to provide 5,755 million dollars, principally for interest. This leaves 24,224 million dollars to be made available through new appropriations, exclusive of appropriations to liquidate contract authorizations; 900 million dollars in new contract authorizations; and 103 million dollars through the reappropriation of unliquidated balances of previous appropriations. The appropriations needed to liquidate contract authorizations are estimated at 1,113 million dollars.

In the Budget for the year ahead only over-all estimates are included at this time for the major war agencies and for net outlays of Government corporations. Detailed recommendations will be transmitted in the spring for the war agencies; and the business-type budgets of Government corporations will likewise be transmitted in accordance with the recently adopted Government Corporation Control Act.

Similarly, only over-all estimates are provided for new programs recommended in this Message; detailed recommendations will be transmitted after authorizing legislation has been enacted. It should be recognized that many of the estimates for new programs recommended in this Message are initial year figures. These figures will be affected by the date the legislation is enacted and by the time needed for getting a program under way. New programs, such as that for a national research agency, will require larger amounts in later years. The estimates exclude major elements of the proposed national health program since the greater part of these will be covered by expenditures from trust funds.

The Budget total includes expenditures for capital outlay as well as for current operations. An estimated 1,740 million dollars will be expended in the fiscal year 1947 for direct Federal public works and for loans and grants for public works.

THE ECONOMIC IMPACT of THE LIQUIDATION

OF THE WAR PROGRAM

Government programs are of such importance in the development of production and employment opportunities—domestic and international—that it has become essential to formulate and consider the Federal Budget in the light of the Nation's budget as a whole. The relationship between the receipts, expenditures, and savings of consumers, business, and government is shown in the accompanying table.

Considering the whole Nation, total expenditures must equal the total receipts, because what any individual or group spends becomes receipts of other individuals or groups. Such equality can be achieved on either a high level of incomes or on a low or depression level of incomes.

Tremendous orders for munitions during the war shifted production and employment into high gear. Total goods produced and services rendered for private as well as for Government purposes—the Nation's budget-reached about 200 billion dollars in the calendar year 1944. Federal, State, and local government expenditures represented half of this total.

Corresponding estimates for the past 3 months depict the

national economy in the process of demobilization and reconversion.

The wartime annual rate of Federal expenditures has been reduced by 32 billion dollars, while the Nation's budget total has dropped only half as much. The drop in total value of production and services has been less drastic because increasing private activities have absorbed in large measure the manpower and materials released from war production and war services.

The largest increase in private activities has occurred in business investments, which include residential and other construction, producers' durable equipment, accumulation of inventories, and net exports. Under conditions of global war, expenditures for private construction and equipment were held to a minimum and inventories were depleted. With the beginning of reconversion these developments have been reversed. Residential construction and outlays for plant and equipment are on the increase; inventories, too, are being replenished. International transactions (excluding lend-lease and international relief which are included under war expenditures) showed an import surplus under conditions of global war. In the past 3 months private exports have been slightly in excess of imports, for the first time since 1941.

Consumers' budgets show a significant change. On the income side, their total has declined but little because the reduction in "take-home" pay of war workers is, to a large extent, offset for the time being by the mustering-out payments received by war veterans and by unemployment compensation received by the unemployed. On the expenditure side, however, consumers' budgets, restricted during the war, have in creased substantially as a result of the fact that scarce goods are beginning to appear on the market and wartime restraints are disappearing. Thus, consumers' current savings are declining substantially from the extraordinarily high wartime rate and some wartime savings are beginning to be used for long-delayed purchases.

Unemployment has increased less than was expected during this first period of demobilization and reconversion. It is true that 6 million men and women have been discharged from the armed forces since May 1945 and more than 5 million have been laid off from war work. On the other hand, more than a million civilians have been enlisted in the armed forces, a considerable number of war veterans have not immediately sought jobs, and many war workers, especially women, have withdrawn from the labor force. In addition, many industries, and especially service trades which were undermanned during the war, are beginning now, for the first time in years, to recruit an adequate labor force. The reduced workweek has also contributed to the absorption of those released from war service and war work.

In general, the drastic cut in war programs has thrown the economy into lower gear; it has not thrown it out of gear. Our economic machine demonstrates remarkable resiliency, although there are many difficulties that must still be overcome. The rapid termination of war contracts, prompt clearance of unneeded Government-owned equipment from private plants, and other reconversion policies have greatly speeded up the beginning of peacetime work in reconverted plants.

Although the first great shock of demobilization and war-work termination has thus been met better than many observers expected, specific industries and specific regions show much unevenness in the progress of reconversion.

The Quarterly Report of the Director of War Mobilization

and Reconversion analyzes the difficulties in recruiting personnel and obtaining materials that hamper reconversion in certain industries and proposes policies to deal with these situations. The lack of adequate housing is one of the main factors checking the flow of workers into areas where job opportunities exist.

FEDERAL REVENUE, BORROWING, AND THE

PUBLIC DEBT

I. FINANCIAL REQUIREMENTS AND TAX POLICY

Recommendations for tax legislation should be considered not only in the light of the financial requirements of the ensuing year, but also in the light of future years' financial requirements and a full consideration of economic conditions.

Expenditures are estimated at nearly 36 billion dollars in the fiscal year 1947; they can hardly be expected to be reduced to less than 25 billion dollars in subsequent years. Net receipts in the fiscal year 1947 are estimated at 31.5 billion dollars.

Included in this estimate are 2 billion dollars of receipts from disposal and rental of surplus property and 190 million dollars of receipts from renegotiation of wartime contracts. These sources of receipts will disappear in future years. Tax collections for the fiscal year 1947 also will not yet fully reflect the reduction in corporate tax liabilities provided in the Revenue Act of 1945. If the extraordinary receipts from the disposal of surplus property and renegotiation of contracts be disregarded, and if the tax reductions adopted in the Revenue Act of 1945 were fully effective, present tax rates would yield about 27 billion dollars.

These estimates for the fiscal year 1947 are based on the assumption of generally favorable business conditions but not on an income reflecting full employment and the high productivity that we hope to achieve. In future years the present tax system, in conjunction with a full employment level of national income, could be expected to yield more than 30 billion dollars, which is substantially above the anticipated peacetime level of expenditures.

In view of the still extraordinarily large expenditures in the coming year and continuing inflationary pressures, I am making no recommendation for tax reduction at this time.

We have already had a substantial reduction in taxes from wartime peaks. The Revenue Act of 1945 was a major tax-reduction measure. It decreased the total tax load by more than one-sixth, an amount substantially in excess of the reductions proposed by the Secretary of the Treasury to congressional tax committees in October 1945. These proposed reductions were designed to encourage reconversion and peacetime business expansion.

The possibility of further tax reductions must depend on the budgetary situation and the economic situation. The level of anticipated expenditures for the fiscal year 1947 and the volume of outstanding public debt require the maintenance of large revenues.

Moreover, inflationary pressures still appear dangerously powerful, and ill-advised tax reduction would operate to strengthen them still further.

My decision not to recommend additional tax reductions at this time is made in the light of existing economic conditions and prospects.

2. BORROWING AND THE PUBLIC DEBT

The successful conclusion of the Victory loan marked the end of war borrowing and the beginning of the transition to postwar debt management.

Because of the success of the Victory loan,. I am happy to report that the Treasury will not need to borrow any new money from the public during the remainder of the present fiscal year except through regular sales of savings bonds and savings notes. Furthermore, a part of the large cash balance now in the Treasury will be used for debt redemption so that the public debt which now amounts to about 278 billion dollars will decrease by several billion dollars during the next 18 months. The present statutory debt limit of 300 billion dollars will provide an ample margin for all of the public-debt transactions through the fiscal year 1947. The net effect of the excess of expenditures and debt redemption on the Treasury cash balance, as compared with selected previous years, is shown in the following table:

EXCESS Of BUDGET EXPENDITURES, THE PUBLIC DEBT, AND THE TREASURY CASH BALANCE IN SELECTED YEARS

Excess of At end of period

Budget ex- _____

penditures Public Cash bal-

Fiscal Year over receipts debt ance

1940 $3. 9 $43. 0 $1. 9

1945 53. 6 258. 7 24. 7 1946:

July-Dec. 1945 18. 1 278. 1 26. 0

Jan.-June 1946 10. 5 275. 0 11. 9

1947 4. 3 271. 0 3. 2

Although the public debt is expected to decline, a substantial volume of refinancing will be required, because of the large volume of maturing obligations. Redemptions of savings bonds also have been running high in recent months and are expected to remain large for some time. The issuance of savings bonds will be continued. These bonds represent a convenient method of investment for small savers, and also an anti-inflationary method of refinancing. Government agencies and trust funds are expected to buy about 2.5 billion dollars of Government securities during the next 6 months, and 2.8 billion dollars more during the fiscal year 1947. Through these and other debt operations, the distribution of the Federal debt among the various types of public and private owners will change, even though the total is expected to decline.

The interest policies followed in the refinancing operations will have a major impact not only on the provision for interest payments in future budgets, but also on the level of interest rates prevailing in private financing. The average rate of interest on the debt is now a little under 2 percent. Low interest rates will be an important force in promoting the full production and full employment in the postwar period for which we are all striving. Close wartime cooperation between the Treasury Department and the Federal Reserve System has made it possible to finance the most expensive war in history at low and stable rates of interest. This cooperation will continue.

No less important than the level of interest rates paid on the debt is the distribution of its ownership. Of the total debt, more than half represents direct savings of individuals or investments of funds received from individual savings by life insurance companies, mutual savings banks, savings and loan associations, private or Government trust funds, and other agencies.

Most of the remaining debt—more than 100 billion dollars—is held by the commercial banks and the Federal Reserve banks. Heavy purchases by the banks were necessary to provide adequate funds to finance war expenditures. A considerable portion of these obligations are short-term in character and hence will require refinancing in the coming months and years. Since they have been purchased out of newly created bank funds, continuance of the present low rates of interest is entirely appropriate. To do otherwise would merely increase bank profits at the expense of the taxpayer.

The 275-billion dollar debt poses a problem that requires careful consideration in the determination of financial and economic policies. We have learned that the problem, serious as it is, can be managed. Its management will require determined action to keep our Federal Budget in order and to relate our fiscal policies to the requirements of an expanding economy. The more successful we are in achieving full production and full employment the easier it will be to manage the debt and pay for the debt service. Large though the debt is, it is within our economic capacity. The interest charges on it amount to but a small proportion of our national income. The Government is determined, by a resolute policy of economic stabilization, to protect the interests of the millions of American citizens who have invested in its securities.

During the past 6 months the net revenue receipts of the Federal Government have been about 20 billion dollars, almost as much as during the closing 6 months of 1944 when the country was still engaged in all-out warfare. The high level of these receipts reflects the smoothness of the reconversion and particularly the strength of consumer demand. But the receipts so far collected, it must be remembered, do not reflect any of the tax reductions made by the Revenue Act of 1945. These reductions will not have their full effect on the revenue collected until the fiscal year 1948.

It is good to move toward a balanced budget and a start on the retirement of the debt at a time when demand for goods is strong and the business outlook is good. These conditions prevail today. Business is good and there are still powerful forces working in the direction of inflation. This is not the time for tax reduction.

RECOMMENDATIONS FOR SPECIFIC FEDERAL ACTIVITIES

1. WAR LIQUIDATION AND NATIONAL DEFENSE

(a) War expenditures.

The fiscal year 1947 will see a continuance of war liquidation and occupation. During this period we shall also lay the foundation for our peacetime system of national defense.

In the fiscal year that ended on June 30, 1945, almost wholly a period of global warfare, war expenditures amounted to 90.5 billion dollars. For the fiscal year 1946 war expenditures were originally estimated at 70 billion dollars.

That estimate was made a year ago while we were still engaged in global warfare. After victory over Japan this estimate was revised to 50.5 billion dollars. Further cut-backs and accelerated demobilization have made possible an additional reduction in the rate of war spending. During the first 6 months 32.9 billion dollars were spent. It is now estimated that 16.1 billion dollars will be spent during the second 6 months, or a total of 49 billion dollars during the whole fiscal year.

For the fiscal year 1947 it is estimated, tentatively, that expenditures for war liquidation, for occupation, and for national defense will be reduced to 15 billion dollars. The War and Navy Departments are expected to spend 13 billion dollars; expenditures of other agencies, such as the United States Maritime Commission, the War Shipping Administration, and the Office of Price Administration, and payments to the United Nations Relief and Rehabilitation Administration are estimated at 3 billion dollars. Allowing for estimated net receipts of 1 billion dollars arising from war activities of the Reconstruction finance Corporation, the estimated total of war expenditures is 15 billion dollars. At this time only a tentative break-down of the total estimate for war and defense activities can be indicated.

An expenditure of 15 billion dollars for war liquidation, occupation, and national defense is a large sum for a year which begins 10 months after fighting has ended. It is 10 times our expenditures for defense before the war; it amounts to about 10 percent of our expected national income. This estimate reflects the immense job that is involved in winding up a global war effort and stresses the great responsibility that victory has placed upon this country. The large expenditures needed for our national defense emphasize the great scope for effective organization in furthering economy and efficiency. To this end I have recently recommended to the Congress adoption of legislation combining the War and Navy Departments into a single Department of National Defense.

A large part of these expenditures is still to be attributed to the costs of the war. Assuming, somewhat arbitrarily, that about one-half of the 15-billion-dollar outlay for the fiscal year 1947 is for war liquidation, aggregate expenditures by this Government for the second World War are now estimated at 347 billion dollars through June 30, 1947. Of this, about 9 billion dollars will have been recovered through renegotiation and sale of surplus property by June 30, 1947; this has been reflected in the estimates of receipts.

Demobilization and strength of armed forces.—Demobilization of our armed forces is proceeding rapidly. At the time of victory in Europe, about 12.3 million men and women were in the armed forces; 7.6 million were overseas. By the end of December 1945 our armed forces had been reduced to below 7 million. By June 30, 1946, they will number about 2.9 million, of whom 1.8 million will be individuals enlisted and inducted after VE-day. Mustering-out pay is a large item of our war liquidation expense; it will total 2.5 billion dollars in the fiscal year 1946, and about 500 million dollars in the fiscal year 1947.

In the fiscal year 1947 the strength of our armed forces will still be above the ultimate peacetime level. As I have said, War and Navy Department requirements indicate a strength of about 2 million in the armed forces a year from now. This is necessary to enable us to do our share in the occupation of enemy territories and in the preservation of peace in a troubled world. Expenditures for pay, subsistence, travel, and miscellaneous expenses of the armed forces, excluding mustering-out pay, are estimated at 5 billion dollars.

Contract settlement and surplus property disposal.—The winding up of war procurement is the second most important liquidation job. By the end of November a total of 301,000 prime contracts involving commitments of 64 billion dollars had been terminated. Of this total, 67,000 contracts with commitments of 35 billion dollars remained to be settled. Termination payments on these contracts are estimated at about 3.5 billion dollars. It is expected that more than half of these terminated contracts will be settled during the current fiscal year, leaving payments of about 1.5 billion dollars for the fiscal year 1947.

Another important aspect of war supply liquidation is the disposal of surplus property. Munitions, ships, plants, installations, and supplies, originally costing 50 billion dollars or more, will ultimately be declared surplus. The sale value of this property will be far less than original cost and disposal expenses are estimated at 10 to 15 cents on each dollar realized. Disposal units within existing agencies have been organized to liquidate surplus property under the direction of the Surplus Property Administration. Overseas disposal activities have been centralized in the State Department to permit this program to be carried on in line with over-all foreign policy. Thus far only about 13 billion dollars of the ultimate surplus, including 5 billion dollars of unsalable aircraft, has been declared. Of this amount, 2.3 billion dollars have been disposed of, in sales yielding 600 million dollars. The tremendous job of handling surplus stocks will continue to affect Federal expenditures and receipts for several years. The speed and effectiveness of surplus disposal operations will be of great importance for the domestic economy as well as for foreign economic policies.

War supplies, maintenance, and relief.-Adequate provision for the national defense requires that we keep abreast of scientific and technical advances. The tentative estimates for the fiscal year 1947 make allowance for military research, limited procurement of weapons in the developmental state, and some regular procurement of munitions which were developed but not mass-produced when the war ended. Expenditures for procurement and construction will constitute one-third or less of total defense outlays, compared to a ratio of two-thirds during the war years.

The estimates also provide for the maintenance of our war-expanded naval and merchant fleets, military installations, and stocks of military equipment and supplies. Our naval combatant fleet is three times its pre-Pearl Harbor tonnage. Our Merchant Marine is five times its prewar size. The War Department has billions of dollars worth of equipment and supplies. Considerable maintenance and repair expense is necessary for the equipment which we desire to retain in active status or in war reserve. Expenses will be incurred for winnowing the stocks of surpluses, for preparing lay-up facilities for the reserve fleets, and for storage of reserve equipment and supplies.

Military expenditures .in the current fiscal year include 650 million dollars for civilian supplies for the prevention of starvation and disease in occupied areas. Expenditures on this account will continue in the fiscal year 1947. The war expenditures also cover the expenses of civilian administration in occupied areas.

During the war, 15 cents of each dollar of our war expenditures was for lend-lease aid. With lend-lease terminated, I expect the direct operations under this program to be substantially completed in the current fiscal year. The expenditures estimated for the fiscal year 1947 under this program are mainly interagency reimbursements for past transactions.

Relief and rehabilitation expenditures are increasing. It is imperative that we give all necessary aid within our means to the people who have borne the ravages of war. I estimate that in the fiscal year 1946 expenditures for the United Nations Relief and Rehabilitation Administration will total 1.3 billion dollars and in the following year 1.2 billion dollars. Insofar as possible, procurement for this purpose will be from war surpluses.

(b) Authorizations for war and national defense.

During the war, authorizations and appropriations had to be enacted well in advance of obligation and spending to afford ample time for planning of production by the procurement services and by industry. Thus our cumulative war program authorized in the period between July 1, 1940, and July 1, 1945, was 431 billion dollars, including net war commitments of Government corporations. Expenditures against those authorizations totaled 290 billion dollars. This left 141 billion dollars in unobligated authorizations and unliquidated obligations.

With the end of fighting, it became necessary to adjust war authorizations to the requirements of war liquidation and continuing national defense. Intensive review of the war authorizations by both the executive and the legislative branches has been continued since VJ-day. As a result, the authorized war program is being brought more nearly into line with expenditures.

Recisions and authorizations through the fiscal year 1946.—Readjusting the war program, as the Congress well knows, is not an easy task. Authorizations must not be too tight, lest we hamper necessary operations; they must not be too ample, lest we lose control of spending. Last September,

I transmitted to the Congress recommendations on the basis of which the Congress voted H.R. 4407 to repeal 50.3 billion dollars of appropriations and authorizations. I found it necessary to veto this bill because it was used as a vehicle for legislation that would impair the reemployment program. However, in order to preserve the fine work of the Congress on the recisions, I asked the Director of the Bureau of the Budget to place the exact amounts indicated for repeal in a nonexpendable reserve, and to advise the departments and agencies accordingly. This has been done.

In accord with Public Law 132 of the Seventy-ninth Congress, I have transmitted recommendations for additional rescissions for the current fiscal year of appropriations amounting to 5.8 billion dollars and of contract authorizations totaling 420 million dollars. The net reduction in authority to obligate will be 5.0 billion dollars, because, of the appropriations, 1.2 billion dollars will have to be restored in subsequent years to liquidate contract authorizations still on the books.

The appropriations recommended for repeal include 2,827 million dollars for the Navy Department, 1,421 million dollars for the War Department, 850 million dollars for lend-lease, 384 million dollars for the War Shipping Administration, and 260 million dollars for the United States Maritime Commission. The contract authorizations proposed for repeal are for the Maritime Commission.

In addition, there are unused tonnage authorizations for construction of naval vessels now valued at 5.4 billion dollars. In September 1945, I suggested that this authority be reviewed by the appropriate committees of the Congress, and the Congress has moved to bar construction under these authorizations during the remainder of the fiscal year 1946. I propose to continue this prohibition in the Navy budget estimates for the fiscal year 1947 and now renew my recommendation that legislation be enacted at the earliest time to dear the statute books of these authorizations.

The amounts indicated for repeal in H.R. 4407 and the further rescissions which I have recommended, excluding duplications and deferred cash payments on existing authorizations, represent a cut in the authorized war program of 60.8 billion dollars. The war authorizations will also be reduced 3'7 billion dollars by carrying receipts of revolving accounts to surplus, by lapses, and by cancelation and repayment of commitments of the Government war corporations.

On the other hand, supplemental appropriations of 600 million dollars will be required for the United Nations Relief and Rehabilitation Administration.

In the net, it is estimated that the cumulative authorized war and national defense program will amount to 368 billion dollars on June 30, 1946. Expenditures of 49 billion dollars during the fiscal year 1946 will have pushed cumulative expenditures to 339 billion dollars. The unexpended balances will be down to 28 billion dollars on June 30, 1946.

New authorizations for national defense and war liquidation in the fiscal year 1947.-The expenditures of 15 billion dollars for national defense and war liquidation in the fiscal year 1947 will be partly for payment of contractual obligations incurred in the past, and partly for the payment of new obligations. The unexpended balances on June 30, 1946, will be scattered among hundreds of separate appropriations. Thus, while some appropriation accounts will have unused balances, others will require additional appropriations.

It is estimated that authorizations to incur new obligations of 11,772 million dollars will be needed during the fiscal year 1947, mainly for the War and Navy Departments. Of the required authorizations, 11,365 million dollars will be in new appropriations, 400 million dollars in new contract authority, and 7 million dollars in reappropriations of unobligated balances. In addition, appropriations of 825 million dollars will be needed to liquidate obligations under existing contract authorizations.

Taking into account the tentative authorizations and expenditures estimated for the fiscal year 1947, and offsets of 3 billion dollars in war commitments of Government corporations, the cumulative authorized war and national defense program on June 30, 1947, will be 376 billion dollars; total expenditures, 354 billion dollars; and unexpended balances, 22 billion dollars.

The 22 billion dollars of unexpended balances tentatively indicated as of June 30, 1947, comprise both unobligated authorizations and unliquidated obligations. Most of the unliquidated obligations result from transactions booked during the war years. A large part of the 22 billion dollars would never be spent even if not repealed, for the appropriations will lapse in due course. For example, several billion dollars of these unliquidated obligations represent unsettled inter- and intra-departmental agency accounts for war procurement. Legislation is being requested to facilitate the adjustment of some of these inter-agency accounts. Another 6 billion dollars is set aside for contract termination payments. If contract settlement costs continue in line with recent experience, it is likely that part of the 6 billion dollars will remain unspent.

On the other hand, some of the 22 billion dollars would be available for obligation and expenditure unless impounded.

In certain appropriations, such as those for long-cycle procurement, considerable carry-over of unliquidated obligations into future years is to be expected and is necessary. However, substantial further rescissions can and should be made when the war liquidation program tapers off and budgetary requirements for national defense are clarified. As I have said, I shall continue to review the war authorizations and from time to time recommend excess balances for repeal.

As in recent years, detailed recommendations concerning most appropriations for the national defense program are postponed until the spring. In connection with the war activities of the United States Maritime Commission and certain other agencies, however, I now make specific recommendations for the fiscal year 1947. No additional authorizations or appropriations will be necessary for the Maritime Commission since sufficient balances will be left after the abovementioned rescissions to carry out the program now contemplated for the fiscal year 1947.

2. AFTERMATH OF WAR

Nearly one-third—11 billion dollars—of estimated Federal expenditures in the fiscal year 1947 will be for purposes that are largely inherited from the war—payments to veterans, interest on the Federal debt, and refunds of taxes.

(a) For veterans.

"Veterans' pensions and benefits" has become one of the largest single categories in the Federal Budget. I am recommending for this purpose total appropriations of 4,787 million dollars for the fiscal year 1947· Expenditures in the fiscal year are estimated, under present legislation, at 4,208 million dollars. These expenditures will help our veterans through their readjustment period and provide lasting care for those who were disabled.

The Congress has provided unemployment allowances for veterans during their readjustment period. Expenditure of 850 million dollars for this purpose is anticipated for the fiscal year 1947. In addition, readjustment allowances for self-employed veterans are expected to cost 340 million dollars in the fiscal year 1947.

On May 28, 1945, in asking the Congress to raise the ceiling on benefits for civilian unemployed to not less than 25 dollars a week during the immediate reconversion period, I suggested that the Congress also consider liberalizing veterans' allowances. Elsewhere in this Message I reiterate my recommendation with respect to emergency unemployment compensation. I also recommend increasing veterans' unemployment allowances from 20 dollars to 25 dollars a week. This would involve additional expenditures estimated at approximately 220 million dollars for the fiscal year.

Included in the 1947 Budget is an expenditure of 535 million dollars for veterans' education under provisions of the Servicemen's Readjustment Act. This amount includes both tuition expenses and maintenance allowances. It is expected that half a million veterans will be enrolled in our schools and colleges during the year.

The ultimate benefit which veterans receive from the loan guarantee provisions of the Servicemen's Readjustment Act depends largely on the success of our stabilization program in restraining building costs and real estate values. Under the revised procedure contained in recent amendments, the administrative workload will be minimized by the almost complete transfer of authority for approving the guarantees to private lending agencies and private appraisers designated by the Veterans Administration. This authority carries with it the responsibility for restricting the guarantees to loans on reasonably valued properties. Costs of the program, other than for administration, are estimated at 21 million dollars in the fiscal year 1947.

Pensions for veterans will require expenditures estimated at 1,748 million dollars for the fiscal year 1947. Two-thirds of this amount will be received by veterans of the war which we have just won. This figure includes 55 million dollars of increased pensions for student-veterans in our vocational rehabilitation program. In addition, 170 million dollars will be expended in transfers to the National Service Life Insurance fund from general and special accounts.

Expenditures under the appropriation for salaries and expenses of the Veterans Administration are estimated at 528 million dollars in the fiscal year 1947. This includes 260 million dollars for medical care and the operation of some 103,000 hospital and domiciliary beds.

A separate appropriation for hospital and domiciliary facilities, additional to the total for veterans' pensions and benefits, covers construction that will provide some 13,000 hospital beds as part of the 500-million dollar hospital construction program already authorized by the Congress. The estimated expenditures of 130 million dollars for this purpose are classified in the Budget as part of the general public works program for the next fiscal year.

(b) For interest.

Interest payments on the public debt are estimated at 5 billion dollars in the fiscal year 1947, an increase of 250 million dollars from the revised estimate for the current fiscal year. This increase reflects chiefly payment of interest on additions to the debt this year. Assuming continuance of present interest rates, the Government's interest bill is now reaching the probable postwar level.

(c) For refunds.

An estimated total of 1,585 million dollars of refunds will be paid to individuals and corporations during the fiscal year 1947. Slightly over half of this amount, or 800 million dollars, will be accessory to the simplified pay-as-you-go method of tax collection, and will be the result of overwithholding and over declaration of expected income. Most of the remainder will arise from loss and excess-profits credit carrybacks, recomputed amortization on war plants, and special relief from the excess profits tax.

This category of expenditures is thus losing gradually its "aftermath-of-war" character, and by the succeeding year will reflect almost entirely the normal operation of loss carry-backs and current tax collection.

3. AGRICULTURAL PROGRAMS

The agricultural programs contemplated for the fiscal year 1947 are those which are essential for the provision of an adequate supply of food and other agricultural commodities with a fair return to American farmers. To support these objectives, expenditures by the Department of Agriculture estimated at 784 million dollars from general and special accounts will be required in the fiscal year 1947. This compares with estimated expenditures of 676 million dollars in 1946. These figures exclude expenditures by the Department of Agriculture on account of lend-lease, the United Nations Relief and Rehabilitation Administration, and other war expenditures. The expenditure for the fiscal year 1947 is composed of 553 million dollars for "aids to agriculture," 35 million dollars for general public works, and 196 million dollars for other services of the Department.

Net outlays for the price stabilization, price support, and other programs of the Commodity Credit Corporation are expected to increase from about 750 million dollars in the fiscal year 1946 to about 1,500 million dollars in 1947. Cash advances made on loans by the farm Security Administration and the Rural Electrification Administration are expected to amount to 266 million dollars in the fiscal year 1946 and 351 million dollars in 1947; and after receipts from principal and interest are taken into account, net loan expenditures of these two agencies will amount to 120 and 209 million dollars in the two fiscal years.

To provide for the expenditures from general and special accounts, I recommend for the fiscal year 1947 appropriations of million dollars (including the existing permanent appropriation of an amount equal to 30 percent of estimated annual customs receipts) and a reappropriation of 88 million dollars of prior-year balances from customs receipts. In addition there is a recommended authorization of 367.5 million dollars for borrowing from the Reconstruction finance Corporation for the loan programs of the farm Security Administration and the Rural Electrification Administration. It is expected that the operations of the Commodity Credit Corporation will be financed during the coming year through the 500 million dollars of lend-lease funds which the Congress has earmarked for price support purposes, a supplemental appropriation to restore impaired capital of the Corporation, and the borrowing authority of the Corporation.

Some detailed recommendations follow for major agricultural programs.

Conservation and use of land.—I am recommending that 270 million dollars be appropriated for "conservation and use of agricultural land resources"—the so-called AAA program—for the fiscal year 1947, compared with 356 million dollars in the current year. This reduction of 86 million dollars is in large part accounted for by elimination of the wartime flax production incentive project and other nonrecurring items; the proposed reduction in normal activities is less than 33 million dollars.

For the past several years, this program has consisted largely of payments to farmers for application of fertilizer and other approved soil management practices. I am convinced that farmers generally are now fully alert to the benefits, both immediate and long-term, which they derive from the practices encouraged by this program. I believe, therefore, that this subsidization should continue to be reduced.

Rural electrification.—It is proposed that the loan authorization for the Rural Electrification Administration for the fiscal year 1947 be increased from 200 million dollars to 250 million dollars. During the war period, REA was limited by the scarcity of materials and manpower. But that situation is rapidly changing, and the REA program, which was materially stepped up for the fiscal year 1946, can be increased still more. It is my belief that a feasible and practical rural electrification program should be carried forward as rapidly as possible. This will involve total loans of approximately 1,800 million dollars over the next 10 years, much of which will be repaid during that period.

Other programs.—It is recommended that the continuing forest land-acquisition program be resumed at the rate of 3 million dollars annually, which is about the minimum rate at which this program can be economically carried on. The lands involved in this program can contribute fully to the national welfare only when brought into the national forest system for protection and development.

Such programs as those of the farm Security Administration and the farm Credit Administration are estimated to be continued during the fiscal year 1947 at about the same level as in the fiscal year 1946. Recent action by the Congress has Permitted some expansion of the school lunch program. I hope it will be continued and expanded. The budgets of the Federal Crop Insurance Corporation and the federal farm Mortgage Corporation will be transmitted in the spring under the terms of the Government Corporation Control Act.

4. TRANSPORTATION

Transportation is one of the major fields for both public and private investment. Our facilities for transportation and communication must be constantly improved to serve better the convenience of the public and to facilitate the sound growth and development of the whole economy.

Federal capital outlays for transportation facilities are expected to approximate 519 million dollars in the fiscal year 1947. State and local governments may spend 400 million dollars. Private investment, over half of it by railways, may approach 1,150 million dollars.

The Congress has already taken steps for the resumption of work on improvement of rivers and harbors and on the construction of new Federal-aid highways. Much needed work on airports can begin when the Congress enacts legislation now in conference between the two Houses.

The Federal expenditure estimates for the fiscal year 1947 include 53 million dollars for new construction in rivers, harbors, and the Panama Canal and 291 million dollars for highways and grade-crossing elimination, assuming that the States expend some 275 million dollars on the Federal-aid system. Additional expenditures for highways totaling 36 million dollars are anticipated by the forest Service, National Park Service, and the Territory of Alaska. Civil airways and airports will involve expenditures of 35 million dollars under existing authority. Additional Federal expenditures exceeding 20 million dollars (to be matched by States and municipalities) may be made during the fiscal year 1947 under the airport legislation now in conference between the two Houses of the Congress.

The United States now controls almost two-thirds of the world's merchant shipping, most of it Government-owned, compared with little more than one-seventh of the world's tonnage in 1939. This places a heavy responsibility upon the Nation to provide for speedy and efficient world commerce as a contribution to general economic recovery.

The estimates for the United States Maritime Commission and War Shipping Administration provide for the transition of shipping operation from a war to a peace basis; the sale, chartering, or lay-up of much of the war-built fleet; and for a program of ship construction of some 84 million dollars in the fiscal year 1947 to round out the merchant fleet for peacetime use.

Federal aids, subsidies, and regulatory controls for transportation should follow the general principle of benefiting the national economy as a whole. They should seek to improve the transportation system and increase its efficiency with resulting lower rates and superior service. Differential treatment which benefits one type of transportation to the detriment of another should be avoided save when it is demonstrated clearly to be in the public interest.

5. RESOURCE DEVELOPMENT

Total capital outlays for resource development are estimated at 653 million dollars in the fiscal year 1947 as compared with 452 million dollars in 1946. These include capital expenditures by the Rural Electrification Administration and expenditures for resource development by other organizational units in the Department of Agriculture which are also mentioned above under "agricultural programs."

The reclamation and flood control projects which I am recommending for the fiscal year 1947 will involve capital outlays of approximately 319 million dollars as compared with 245 million dollars in the fiscal year 1946. These expenditures cover programs of the Corps of Engineers, the Bureau of Reclamation, the Bureau of Indian Affairs, the Department of Agriculture, and the International Boundary and Water Commission, United States and Mexico. A number of these projects are multiple-purpose projects, providing not only for reclamation and irrigation of barren land and flood control, but also for the production of power needed for industrial development of the areas.

Expenditures for power transmission and distribution facilities by the Bonneville Power Administration are expected to increase from 12 million dollars in the fiscal year 1946 to 15 million dollars in the next fiscal year. In addition, the Southwestern Power Administration will undertake a new program involving expenditures of about 16 million dollars in the fiscal year 1947. The Rural Electrification Administration will require expenditures during the current fiscal year estimated at 156 million dollars; in the fiscal year 1947, at 241 million dollars.

The TVA program includes completion of major multiple-purpose projects—navigation, flood control, and power facilities—and additions to chemical plants and related facilities. Expenditures for these capital improvement programs are estimated at 30 million dollars in the fiscal year 1946 and 39 million dollars in the fiscal year 1947.

Expenditures for construction of roads and other developmental works in the national forests, parks, and other public lands, and for capital outlays for fish and wildlife development will increase from below 9 million dollars in the fiscal year 1946 to 24 million dollars in the fiscal year 1947.

6. SOCIAL SECURITY AND HEALTH

Benefit payments out of the Old-Age and Survivors Insurance Trust fund during 1947 are estimated at 407 million dollars, while withdrawals by the States from the Unemployment Trust fund for compensation payments are expected to total 1 billion dollars. These disbursements are financed out of social security contributions.

The appropriations from general and special accounts for the social security program, which cover Federal administrative expenses and grants to States for assistance programs, are estimated at 593 million dollars for the fiscal year 1947, an increase of 57 million dollars over the current year. The increase anticipates greater administrative workload and higher grants to match increasing State payments. The social security program does not include all the Federal health services under existing legislation. For the other health services classified under general government and national defense, appropriations are estimated at 102 million dollars for the fiscal year 1947.

Some expansion in peacetime medical research and other programs of the Public Health Service is provided for in the appropriation estimates for these purposes totaling approximately 87 million dollars for the fiscal year 1947 which are submitted under provisions of existing law. Part of this will be provided through the social security appropriations, the remainder through other appropriations. About 28 million dollars is recommended for maternity care and health services for children under existing law, mainly under the emergency provision for the wives and infants of servicemen. While we should avoid duplication of maternity and child health services which will be provided through the proposed general system of prepaid medical care, legislation is needed to supplement such services. For medical education, I have recommended legislation authorizing grants-in-aid to public and nonprofit institutions. The existing sources of support for medical schools require supplementation to sustain the expansion that is needed.

Hospitals, sanitation works, and additional facilities at medical schools will be required for an adequate national health program. Legislation is now pending in the Congress to authorize grants for the construction of hospitals and health centers and grants and loans for water-pollution control. I hope the Congress will act favorably on generous authorizing legislation.

7. RESEARCH AND EDUCATION

The Budget provides for continuation and desirable expansion of the research activities that are carried on throughout the Federal establishment and through previously authorized grants to the States. Additional appropriations will be required for the proposed central Federal research agency which I recommended last

September 6. That agency will coordinate existing research activities and administer funds for new research activities wherever they are needed; it will not itself conduct research. The plan contemplates expenditures through the new research agency of approximately 40 million dollars for the first year.

These amounts are small in relation to the important contribution they can make to the national income, the welfare of our people, and the common defense. Expenditures must be limited for the time being by the capacity of research agencies to make wise use of funds. The maintenance of our position as a nation, however, will require more emphasis on research expenditures in the future than in the past.

Educational expenditures will require a significant share of the national income in the fiscal year 1947. State, local, and private expenditures for the current support of elementary, secondary, and higher education are expected to be substantially above 3 billion dollars in that year. These nonfederal expenditures will be supplemented by Federal expenditures estimated at 625 million dollars in the present Budget. Of this amount, the estimate for veterans' education, as previously mentioned, is 535 million dollars. Other amounts include 21 million dollars for the support of vocational education in public schools, 5 million dollars for the land-grant colleges, 50 million dollars for the present school-lunch and milk program, 1 million dollars for the Office of Education, and approximately 13 million dollars for various other items. In view of the major policy issues which are still under study by the Congress and the Administration, no specific amount has been determined for the Federal grants, previously recommended in this Message, which would assist the States generally in assuring more nearly equal opportunities for a good education.

Notwithstanding the urgent need for additional school and college buildings, careful planning will be required for the expenditures to be made under the proposed legislation to aid the States in providing educational facilities. A major share of the grants for the first year would be for surveys and plans.

I have already outlined the broad objectives of our foreign economic policy. In the present section I shall indicate the Federal outlays which the execution of these programs may require in the fiscal years 1946 and 1947.

(a) On the termination of lend-lease, the lend-lease countries were required to pay for goods in the lend-lease pipe line either in cash or by borrowing from the United States or by supplying goods and services to the United States. Credits for this purpose have already been extended to Soviet Union, France, the Netherlands, and Belgium amounting to 675 million dollars. The settlement credit of 650 million dollars to the United Kingdom includes an amount preliminarily fixed at 118 million dollars which represents the excess of purchases by the United Kingdom from the pipe line over goods and services supplied by the United Kingdom to the United States since VJ-day and the balance of various claims by one government against the other.

Credits are also being negotiated with lend-lease countries to finance the disposition of lend-lease inventories and installations and property declared to be surplus. For instance, 532 million dollars of the settlement credit to the United Kingdom is for this purpose. These credits will involve no new expenditures by this Government, since they merely provide for deferred repayment by other governments for good: services which have been financed from war appropriations.

(b) Expenditures from the appropriations to United Nations Relief and Rehabilitation Administration, which were discarded under war expenditures above, are estimated to be 1.3 billion dollars in the fiscal year 1946 and 1.2 billion dollars in the fiscal year 1947.

(c) To assist other countries in the restoration of their economies the Export-Import Bank has already negotiated loans in the fiscal year 1946 amounting in total to about 1,010 million dollars and an additional 195 million dollars will probably be committed shortly. The Bank is also granting loans to carry out its original purpose of directly expanding the foreign trade of the United States. In this connection the Bank has established a fund of 100 million dollars to finance the export of cotton from the United States. The Export-Import Bank has thus loaned or committed approximately 1,300 million dollars during the current fiscal year and it is expected that demands on its resources will increase in the last 6 months of the fiscal year 1946. Requests for loans are constantly being received by the Bank from countries desiring to secure goods and services in this country for the reconstruction or development of their economies. On July 31, 1945, the lending authority of the Expert-Import Bank was increased to a total of 3,500 million dollars. I anticipate that during the period covered by this Budget the Bank will reach this limit. The bulk of the expenditures from the loans already granted will fall in the fiscal year 1946 while the bulk of the expenditures from loans yet to be negotiated will fall in the fiscal year 1947. In view of the urgent need for the Bank's credit, I may find it necessary to request a further increase in its lending authority at a later date.

(d) The proposed line of credit of 3,750 million dollars to the United Kingdom will be available up to the end of 1951 and will be used to assist the United Kingdom in financing the deficit in its balance of payments during the transition period. The rate at which the United Kingdom will draw on the credit will depend on the rapidity with which it can reconvert its economy and adapt its trade to the postwar world. The anticipated rate of expenditure is likely to be heaviest during the next 2 years.

(e) Since the Bretton Woods Agreements have now been approved by the required number of countries, both the International Monetary fund and the International Bank for Reconstruction and Development will commence operations during 1946. The organization of these institutions will undoubtedly take some time, and it is unlikely that their operations will reach any appreciable scale before the beginning of the fiscal year 1947.

Of the 2,750 million dollars required for the fund, 1,800 million dollars will be provided in cash or notes from the exchange stabilization fund established under the Gold Reserve Act of 1934. The remaining 950 million dollars will be paid initially in the form of non-interest-bearing notes issued by the Secretary of the Treasury. It is not anticipated that the fund will require in cash any of the 950 million dollars during the fiscal years 1946 and 1947. Consequently, no cash withdrawals from the Treasury will be required in connection with the fund in these years.

The subscription to the Bank amounts to 3,175 million dollars. Of this total, 2 percent must be paid immediately and the Bank is required to call a further 8 percent of the subscription during its first year of operations. The balance of the subscription is payable when required by the Bank either for direct lending or to make good its guarantees. It is likely that the United States will be required to pay little if any more than the initial 10 percent before the end of the fiscal year 1947.

I anticipate that net expenditures of the Export-Import Bank and expenditures arising from the British credit and the Bretton Woods Agreements will amount to 2,614 million dollars, including the noncash item of 950 million dollars for the fund, in the fiscal year 1946, and 2,754 million dollars in the fiscal year 1947.

GENERAL GOVERNMENT

The responsibilities of the Government, in both domestic and international affairs, have increased greatly in the past decade. Consequently, the Government is larger than it was before the war, and its general operating costs are higher. We cannot shrink the Government to prewar dimensions unless we slough off these new responsibilities—and we cannot do that without paying an excessive price in terms of our national welfare. We can, however, enhance its operating efficiency through improved organization. I expect to make such improvements under the authority of the Reorganization Act of 1945.

The appropriations which I am recommending for general government for the fiscal year 1947 are 1,604 million dollars under existing legislation. This is an increase of 458 million dollars over the total of enacted appropriations for the current fiscal year, but a substantial part of this increase is due to the fact that the appropriations for the fiscal year 1946 were made prior to the general increase of employees' salaries last July 1, for which allowance is made in the anticipated supplemental appropriations for 1946. The recommended total for 1947 for general government, like the estimates for national defense and other specific programs, does not allow for the further salary increases for Government employees which, I hope, will be authorized by pending legislation, but-the tentative lump-sum estimates under proposed legislation contemplate that such salary increases will be effective almost at once.

Expenditures for general government in the fiscal year 1947 are expected to continue the slowly rising trend which began in 1943. This category includes a great variety of items—not merely the overhead costs of the Government. It includes all the expenditures of the Cabinet departments, other than for national defense, aids to agriculture, general public works, and the social security program. It includes also expenditures of the legislative branch, the Judiciary, and many of the independent agencies of the executive branch. Consequently, the estimated increase in 1947 in the total of general government expenditures reflects a variety of influences.

Now included in general government are certain activities formerly classified under national defense. Some of these, such as certain functions of the former foreign Economic Administration and the War Manpower Commission, are still needed during the period of reconversion; others are in the process of liquidation. A few wartime activities, for example, the international information and foreign intelligence services and some of the wartime programs for controlling disease and crime, have become part of our regular government establishment. Expenditures for these former wartime functions explain about 40 percent of the increase in expenditures for general government.

Other increases are for civil aeronautics promotion, the business and manufacturing censuses, and other expanded business services of the Department of Commerce which have been referred to above; the forest and Soil Conservation Services and other committees of the Department of certain conservation activities of the

Department of the Interior; and the collection of internal revenue in the Treasury Department.

The necessity for reestablishing postal services curtailed during the war and advances in the rates of pay for postal employees have increased substantially the estimated expenditures for postal service for both the current and the next fiscal year. It is not expected that this increase will cause expenditures to exceed postal revenues in either year, although an excess of expenditures may occur in the fiscal year 1947 if salaries are increased further.

Expenditures for our share of the administrative budgets of the United Nations and other permanent international bodies will increase sharply in the fiscal year 1947, yet will remain a small part of our total Budget. The budget for the United Nations has not yet been determined; an estimate for our contribution will be submitted later. Our contributions to the food and Agriculture Organization, the International Labor Office, the Pan American Union, and other similar international agencies will aggregate about 3 million dollars for the fiscal year 1947. The administrative expenses of the International Monetary fund and the International Bank will be met from their general funds.

We have won a great war—we, the nations of plain people who hate war. In the test of that war we found a strength of unity that brought us through—a strength that crushed the power of those who sought by force to deny our faith in the dignity of man.

During this trial the voices of disunity among us were silent or were subdued to an occasional whine that warned us that they were still among us. Those voices are beginning to cry aloud again. We must learn constantly to turn deaf ears to them. They are voices which foster fear and suspicion and intolerance and hate. They seek to destroy our harmony, our understanding of each other, our American tradition of "live and let live." They have become busy again, trying to set race against race, creed against creed, farmer against city dweller, worker against employer, people against their own governments. They seek only to do us mischief. They must not prevail.

It should be impossible for any man to contemplate without a sense of personal humility the tremendous events of the 12 months since the last annual Message, the great tasks that confront us, the new and huge problems of the coming months and years. Yet these very things justify the deepest confidence in the future of this Nation of free men and women.

The plain people of this country found the courage and the strength, the self-discipline, and the mutual respect to fight and to win, with the help of our allies, under God. I doubt if the tasks of the future are more difficult. But if they are, then I say that our strength and our knowledge and our understanding will be equal to those tasks.

As printed above, references to tables appearing in the budget document have been omitted.

State of the Union Address Harry S. Truman

January 6, 1947

Mr. President, Mr. Speaker, Members of the Congress of the United States:

It looks like a good many of you have moved over to the left since I was here last!

I come before you today to report on the State of the Union and, in the words of the Constitution, to recommend such measures as I judge necessary and expedient.

I come also to welcome you as you take up your duties and to discuss with you the manner in which you and I should fulfill our obligations to the American people during the next 2 years.

The power to mold the future of this Nation lies in our hands—yours and mine, and they are joined together by the Constitution.

If in this year, and in the next, we can find the right course to take as each issue arises, and if, in spite of all difficulties, we have the courage and the resolution to take that course, then we shall achieve a state of well-being for our people without precedent in history. And if we continue to work with the other nations of the world earnestly, patiently, and wisely, we can—granting a will for peace on the part of our neighbors-make a lasting peace for the world.

But, if we are to realize these ends, the Congress and the President, during the next 2 years, must work together. It is not unusual in our history that the majority of the Congress represents a party in opposition to the President's party. I am the twentieth President of the United States who, at some time during his term of office, has found his own party to be in the minority in one or both Houses of Congress. The first one was George Washington. Wilson was number eighteen, and Hoover was number nineteen.

I realize that on some matters the Congress and the President may have honest differences of opinion. Partisan differences, however, did not cause material disagreements as to the conduct of the war. Nor, in the conduct of our international relations, during and since the war, have such partisan differences been material.

On some domestic issues we may, and probably shall, disagree. That in itself is not to be feared. It is inherent in our form of Government. But there are ways of disagreeing; men who differ can still work together sincerely for the common good. We shall be risking the Nation's safety and destroying our opportunities for progress if we do not settle any disagreements in this spirit, without thought of partisan advantage.

THE GENERAL DOMESTIC ECONOMY

As the year 1947 begins, the state of our national economy

presents great opportunities for all. We have virtually full employment. Our national production of goods and services is 50 percent higher than in any year prior to the war emergency. The national income in 1946 was higher than in any peacetime year. Our food production is greater than it has ever been. During the last 5 years our productive facilities have been expanded in almost every field. The American standard of living is higher now than ever before, and when the housing shortage can be overcome it will be even higher.

During the past few months we have removed at a rapid rate the emergency controls that the Federal Government had to exercise during the war. The remaining controls will be retained only as long as they are needed to protect the public. Private enterprise must be given the greatest possible freedom to continue the expansion of economy.

In my proclamation of December 31, 1946 I announced the termination of hostilities. This automatically ended certain temporary legislation and certain executive powers.

Two groups of temporary laws still remain: the first are those which by Congressional mandate are to last during the "emergency"; the second are those which are to continue until the "termination of the war,"

I shall submit to the Congress recommendations for the repeal of certain of the statutes which by their terms continue for the duration of the "emergency." I shall at the same time recommend that others within this classification be extended until the state of war has been ended by treaty or by legislative action. As to those statutes which continue until the state of war has been terminated, I urge that the Congress promptly consider each statute individually, and repeal such emergency legislation where it is advisable.

Now that nearly all wartime controls have been removed, the operation of our industrial system depends to a greater extent on the decisions of businessmen, farmers, and workers. These decisions must be wisely made with genuine concern for public welfare. The welfare of businessmen, farmers, and workers depends upon the economic well-being of those who buy their products.

An important present source of danger to our economy is the possibility that prices might be raised to such an extent that the consuming public could not purchase the tremendous volume of goods and services which will be produced during 1947.

We all know that recent price increases have denied to many of our workers much of the value of recent wage increases. Farmers have found that a large part of their increased income has been absorbed by increased prices. While some of our people have received raises in income which exceed price increases, the great majority have not. Those persons who live on modest fixed incomes—retired persons living on pensions, for example—and workers whose incomes are relatively inflexible, such as teachers and other civil servants—have suffered hardship.

In the effort to bring about a sound and equitable price structure, each group of our population has its own responsibilities.

It is up to industry not only to hold the line on existing prices, but to make reductions whenever profits justify such action.

It is up to labor to refrain from pressing for unjustified wage increases that will force increases in the price level.

And it is up to Government to do everything in its power to encourage high-volume Production, for that is what makes possible good wages, low prices, and reasonable profits.

In a few days there will be submitted to the Congress the Economic Report of the President, and also the Budget Message. Those messages will contain many recommendations. Today I shall outline five major economic policies which I believe the Government should pursue during 1947. These policies are designed to meet our immediate needs and, at the same time, to provide for the long-range welfare of our free enterprise system:

First, the promotion of greater harmony between labor and management.

Second, restriction of monopoly and unfair business practices; assistance to small business; and the promotion of the free competitive system of private enterprise.

Third, continuation of an aggressive program of home construction.

Fourth, the balancing of the budget in the next fiscal year and the achieving of a substantial surplus to be applied to the reduction of the public debt.

Fifth, protection of a fair level of return to farmers in post-war agriculture.

LABOR AND MANAGEMENT

The year just past—like the year after the first World War—was marred by labor management strife.

Despite this outbreak of economic warfare in 1946, we are today producing goods and services in record volume. Nevertheless, it is essential to improve the methods for reaching agreement between labor and management and to reduce the number of strikes and lockouts.

We must not, however, adopt punitive legislation. We must not in order to punish a few labor leaders, pass vindictive laws which will restrict the proper rights of the rank and file of labor. We must not, under the stress of emotion, endanger our American freedoms by taking ill-considered action which will lead to results not anticipated or desired.

We must remember, in reviewing the record of disputes in 1946, that management shares with labor the responsibility for failure to reach agreements which would have averted strikes. For that reason, we must realize that industrial peace cannot be achieved merely by laws directed against labor unions.

During the last decade and a half, we have established a national labor policy in this country based upon free collective bargaining as the process for determining wages and working conditions.

That is still the national policy.

And it should continue to be the national policy!

But as yet, not all of us have learned what it means to bargain freely and fairly. Nor have all of us learned to carry the mutual responsibilities that accompany the right to bargain. There have been abuses and harmful practices which limit the effectiveness of our system of collective bargaining. Furthermore, we have lacked sufficient governmental machinery to aid labor and management in resolving their differences.

Certain labor-management problems need attention at once and certain others, by reason of their complexity, need exhaustive investigation and study.

We should enact legislation to correct certain abuses and to provide additional governmental assistance in bargaining. But we should also concern ourselves with the basic causes of labor-management difficulties.

In the light of these considerations, I propose to you and urge your cooperation in effecting the following four-point program to reduce industrial strife:

Point number one is the early enactment of legislation to prevent certain unjustifiable practices.

First, under this point, are jurisdictional strikes. In such strikes the public and the employer are innocent bystanders who are injured by a collision between rival unions. This type of dispute hurts production, industry, and the public—and labor itself. I consider jurisdictional strikes indefensible.

The National Labor Relations Act provides procedures for determining which union represents employees of a particular employer. In some jurisdictional disputes, however, minority unions strike to compel employers to deal with them despite a legal duty to bargain with the majority union. Strikes to compel an employer to violate the law are inexcusable. Legislation to prevent such strikes is clearly desirable.

Another form of inter-union disagreement is the jurisdictional strike involving the question of which labor union is entitled to perform a particular task. When rival unions are unable to settle such disputes themselves, provision must be made for peaceful and binding determination of the issues.

A second unjustifiable practice is the secondary boycott, when used to further jurisdictional disputes or to compel employers to violate the National Labor Relations Act.

Not all secondary boycotts are unjustified. We must judge them on the basis of their objectives. For example, boycotts intended to protect wage rates and working conditions should be distinguished from those in furtherance of jurisdictional disputes. The structure of industry sometimes requires unions, as a matter of self-preservation, to extend the conflict beyond a particular employer. There should be no blanket prohibition against boycotts. The appropriate goal is legislation which prohibits secondary boycotts in pursuance of unjustifiable objectives, but does not impair the union's right to preserve its own existence and the gains made in genuine collective bargaining.

A third practice that should be corrected is the use of economic force, by either labor or management, to decide issues arising out of the interpretation of existing contracts.

Collective bargaining agreements, like other contracts, should be faithfully adhered to by both parties. In the most enlightened union-management relationships, disputes over the interpretation of contract terms are settled peaceably by negotiation or arbitration. Legislation should be enacted to provide machinery whereby unsettled disputes concerning the interpretation of an existing agreement may be referred by either party to final and binding arbitration.

Point number two is the extension of facilities within the

Department of Labor for assisting collective bargaining.

One of our difficulties in avoiding labor strife arises from a lack of order in the collective bargaining process. The parties often do not have a dear understanding of their responsibility for settling disputes through their own negotiations. We constantly see instances where labor or management resorts to economic force without exhausting the possibilities for agreement through the bargaining process. Neither the parties nor the Government have a definite yardstick for determining when and how Government assistance should be invoked. There is need for integrated governmental machinery to provide the successive steps of mediation, voluntary arbitration, and—ultimately in appropriate cases—ascertainment of the facts of the dispute and the reporting of the facts to the public. Such machinery would facilitate and expedite the settlement of disputes.

Point number three is the broadening of our program of social legislation to alleviate the causes of workers' insecurity.

On June 11, 1946, in my message vetoing the Case Bill, I made a comprehensive statement of my views concerning labor-management relations. I said then, and I repeat now, that the solution of labor-management difficulties is to be found not only in legislation dealing directly with labor relations, but also in a program designed to remove the causes of insecurity felt by many workers in our industrial society. In this connection, for example, the Congress should consider the extension and broadening of our social security system, better housing, a comprehensive national health program, and provision for a fair minimum wage.

Point number four is the appointment of a Temporary Joint

Commission to inquire into the entire field of labor-management relations.

I recommend that the Congress provide for the appointment of a Temporary Joint Commission to undertake this broad study.

The President, the Congress, and management and labor have a continuing responsibility to cooperate in seeking and finding the solution of these problems. I therefore recommend that the Commission be composed as follows: twelve to be chosen by the Congress from members of both parties in the House and the Senate, and eight representing the public, management and labor, to be appointed by the President.

The Commission should be charged with investigating and making recommendations upon certain major subjects, among others:

First, the special and unique problem of nationwide strikes in vital industries affecting the public interest. In particular, the Commission should examine into the question of how to settle or prevent such strikes without endangering our general democratic freedoms.

Upon a proper solution of this problem may depend the whole industrial future of the United States. The paralyzing effects of a nationwide strike in such industries as transportation, coal, oil, steel, or communications can result in national disaster. We have been able to avoid such disaster, in recent years, only by the use of extraordinary war powers. All those powers will soon be gone. In their place there must be created an adequate system and effective machinery in these vital fields. This problem will require careful study and a bold approach, but an approach consistent with the preservation of the rights of our people. The need is pressing. The Commission should give this its earliest attention.

Second, the best methods and procedures for carrying out the collective bargaining process. This should include the responsibilities of labor and management to negotiate freely and fairly with each other, and to refrain from strikes or lockouts until all possibilities of negotiation have been exhausted.

Third, the underlying causes of labor management disputes.

Some of the subjects presented here for investigation involve long-range study. Others can be considered immediately by the Commission and its recommendations can be submitted to the Congress in the near future.

I recommend that this Commission make its first report, including specific legislative recommendations, not later than March 15, 1947.

RESTRICTION Of MONOPOLY AND PROMOTION OF PRIVATE ENTERPRISE

The second major policy I desire to lay before you has to do with the growing concentration of economic power and the threat to free competitive private enterprise. In 1941 the Temporary National Economic Committee completed a comprehensive investigation into the workings of the national economy. The Committee's study showed that, despite a half century of anti-trust law enforcement, one of the gravest threats to our welfare lay in the increasing concentration of power in the hands of a small number of giant organizations.

During the war, this long-standing tendency toward economic concentration was accelerated. As a consequence, we now find that to a greater extent than ever before, whole industries are dominated by one or a few large organizations which can restrict production in the interest of higher profits and thus reduce employment and purchasing power.

In an effort to assure full opportunity and free competition to business we will vigorously enforce the anti-trust laws. There is much the Congress can do to cooperate and assist in this program.

To strengthen and enforce the laws that regulate business practices is not enough. Enforcement must be supplemented by positive measures of aid to new enterprises. Government assistance, research programs, and credit powers should be designed and used to promote the growth of new firms and new industries. Assistance to small business is particularly important at this time when thousands of veterans who are potential business and industrial leaders are beginning their careers.

We should also give special attention to the decentralization of industry and the development of areas that are now under-industrialized. HOUSING

The third major policy is also of great importance to the national economy: an aggressive program to encourage housing construction. The first federal program to relieve the veterans' housing shortage was announced in February 1946. In 1946 one million family housing units have been put under construction and more than 665,000 units have already been completed. The rate of expansion in construction has broken all records.

In the coming year the number of dwelling units built will

approach, if not surpass, the top construction year of 1926. The primary responsibility to deliver housing at reasonable prices that veterans can afford rests with private industry and with labor. The Government will continue to expedite the flow of key building materials, to limit nonresidential construction, and to give financial support where it will do the most good. Measures to stimulate rental housing and new types of housing construction will receive special emphasis.

To reach our long-range goal of adequate housing for all our people, comprehensive housing legislation is urgently required, similar to the non-partisan bill passed by the Senate last year. At a minimum, such legislation should open the way for rebuilding the blighted areas of our cities and should establish positive incentives for the investment of billions of dollars of private capital in large-scale rental housing projects. It should provide for improvement of housing in rural areas and for the construction, over a 4-year period, of half a million units of public low-rental housing. It should authorize a single peacetime federal housing agency to assure efficient use of our resources on the vast housing front.

FISCAL AFFAIRS

The fourth major policy has to do with the balancing of the budget. In a prosperous period such as the present one, the budget of the Federal Government should be balanced. Prudent management of public finance requires that we begin the process of reducing the public debt. The budget which I shall submit to you this week has a small margin of surplus. In the Budget Message I am making recommendations which, if accepted, will result in a substantially larger surplus which should be applied to debt retirement. One of these recommendations is that the

Congress take early action to continue throughout the next fiscal year the war excise tax rates which, under the present law, will expire on June 30, 1947.

Expenditures relating to the war are still high. Considerable sums are required to alleviate world famine and suffering. Aid to veterans will continue at peak level. The world situation is such that large military expenditures are required. Interest on the public debt and certain other costs are irreducible. For these reasons I have had to practice stringent economy in preparing the budget; and I hope that the Congress will cooperate in this program of economy.
AGRICULTURE

The fifth major policy has to do with the welfare of our farm population.

Production of food reached record heights in 1946. Much of our tremendous grain crop can readily be sold abroad and thus will become no threat to our domestic markets. But in the next few years American agriculture can face the same dangers it did after World War I. In the early twenties the Nation failed to maintain outlets for the new productive capacity of our agricultural plant. It failed to provide means to protect the farmer while he adjusted his acreage to peacetime demands.

The result we all remember too well. Farm production stayed up while demand and prices fell, in contrast with industry where prices stayed up and output declined, farm surpluses piled up, and disaster followed.

We must make sure of meeting the problems which we failed to meet after the first World War. Present laws give considerable stability to farm prices for 1947 and 1948, and these 2 years must be utilized to maintain and develop markets for our great productive power.

The purpose of these laws was to permit an orderly transition from war to peace. The Government plan of support prices was not designed to absorb, at great cost, the unlimited surpluses of a highly productive agriculture.

We must not wait until the guarantees expire to set the stage for permanent farm welfare

The farmer is entitled to a fair income.

Ways can be found to utilize his new skills and better practices, to expand his markets at home and abroad, and to carry out the objectives of a balanced pattern of peacetime production without either undue sacrifice by farm people or undue expense to the Government.

HEALTH AND GENERAL WELFARE

Of all our national resources, none is of more basic value than the health of our people. Over a year ago I presented to the Congress my views on a national health program. The Congress acted on several of the recommendations in this program-mental health, the health of mothers and children, and hospital construction. I urge this Congress to complete the work begun last year and to enact the most important recommendation of the program—to provide adequate medical care to all who need it, not as charity but on the basis of payments made by the beneficiaries of the program.

One administrative change would help greatly to further our national program in the fields of health, education, and welfare. I again recommend the establishment of a well-integrated Department of Welfare. VETERANS

Fourteen million World War II servicemen have returned to civil life. The great majority have found their places as citizens of their communities and their Nation. It is a tribute to the fiber of our servicemen and to the flexibility of our economy that these adjustments have been made so rapidly and so successfully.

More than two million of these veterans are attending schools or acquiring job skills through the financial assistance of the Federal Government. Thousands of sick and wounded veterans are daily receiving the best of medical and hospital care. Half a million have obtained loans, with Government guarantees, to purchase homes or farms or to embark upon new businesses. Compensation is being paid in almost two million cases for disabilities or death. More than three million are continuing to mainlain their low-cost National Service Life Insurance policies. Almost seven million veterans have been aided by unemployment and self-employment allowances.

Exclusive of mustering-out payments and terminal leave pay, the program for veterans of all wars is costing over seven billion dollars a year—one-fifth of our total federal budget. This is the most far-reaching and complete veterans program ever conceived by any nation.

Except for minor adjustments, I believe that our program of benefits for veterans is now complete. In the long run, the success of the program will not be measured by the number of veterans receiving financial aid or by the number of dollars we spend. History will judge us not by the money we spend, but by the further contribution we enable our veterans to make to their country. In considering any additional legislation, that must be our criterion.

CIVIL RIGHTS

We have recently witnessed in this country numerous attacks upon the constitutional rights of individual citizens as a result of racial and religious bigotry. Substantial segments of our people have been prevented from exercising fully their right to participate in the election of public officials, both locally and nationally. Freedom to engage in lawful callings has been denied.

The will to fight these crimes should be in the hearts of every one of us.

For the Federal Government that fight is now being carried on by the Department of Justice to the full extent of the powers that have been conferred upon it. While the Constitution withholds from the Federal Government the major task of preserving peace in the several States, I am not convinced that the present legislation reached the limit of federal power to protect the civil rights of its citizens.

I have, therefore, by Executive Order,1 established the President's Committee on Civil Rights to study and report on the whole problem of federally-secured civil rights, with a view to making recommendations to the Congress.

1 Executive Order 9808 (3 CFR, 1943-1948 Comp., p. 590.)

NATURAL RESOURCES

In our responsibility to promote the general welfare of the people, we have always to consider the natural resources of our country. They are the foundation of our life. In the development of the great river systems of America there is the major opportunity of our generation to contribute to the increase of the national wealth. This program is already well along; it should be pushed with full vigor.

I must advise the Congress that we are rapidly becoming a "have not" Nation as to many of our minerals. The economic progress and the security of our country depend upon an expanding return of mineral discovery and upon improved methods of recovery. The Federal Government must do its part to meet this need.

FOREIGN AFFAIRS

Progress in reaching our domestic goals is closely related to our conduct of foreign affairs. All that I have said about maintaining a sound and prosperous economy and improving the welfare of our people has greater meaning because of the world leadership of the United States. What we do, or fail to do, at home affects not only ourselves but millions throughout the world. If we are to fulfill our responsibilities to ourselves and to other peoples, we must make sure that the United States is sound economically, socially, and politically. Only then will we be able to help bring about the elements of peace in other countries—political stability, economic advancement, and social progress.

Peace treaties for Italy, Bulgaria, Rumania, and Hungary have finally been prepared. Following the signing of these treaties next month in Paris, they will be submitted to the Senate for ratification. This Government does not regard the treaties as completely satisfactory. Whatever their defects, however, I am convinced that they are as good as we can hope to obtain by agreement among the principal wartime Allies. Further dispute and delay would gravely jeopardize political stability in the countries concerned for many years.

During the long months of debate on these treaties, we have made it clear to all nations that the United States will not consent to settlements at the expense of principles we regard as vital to a just and enduring peace. We have made it equally clear that we will not retreat to isolationism. Our policies will be the same during the forthcoming negotiations in Moscow on the German and Austrian treaties, and during the future conferences on the Japanese treaty.

The delay in arriving at the first peace settlements is due partly to the difficulty of reaching agreement with the Soviet Union on the terms of settlement. Whatever differences there may have been between us and the Soviet Union, however, should not be allowed to obscure the fact that the basic interests of both nations lie in the early making of a peace under which the peoples of all countries may return, as free men and women, to the essential tasks of production and reconstruction. The major concern of each of us should be the promotion of collective security, not the advancement of individual security.

Our policy toward the Soviet Union is guided by the same principles which determine our policies toward all nations. We seek only to uphold the principles of international justice which have been embodied in the Charter of the United Nations.

We must now get on with the peace settlements. The occupying powers should recognize the independence of Austria and withdraw their troops. The Germans and the Japanese cannot be left in doubt and fear as to their future; they must know their national boundaries, their resources, and what reparations they must pay. Without trying to manage their internal affairs, we can insure that these countries do not re-arm.

INTERNATIONAL RELIEF AND DISPLACED

PERSONS

The United States can be proud of its part in caring for the peoples reduced to want by the ravages of war, and in aiding nations to restore their national economies. We have shipped more supplies to the hungry peoples of the world since the end of the war than all other countries combined!

However, insofar as admitting displaced persons is concerned, I do not feel that the United States has done its part. Only about 5,000 of them have entered this country since May, 1946. The fact is that the executive agencies are now doing all that is reasonably possible under the limitation of the existing law and established quotas. Congressional assistance in the form of new legislation is needed. I urge the Congress to turn its attention to this world problem, in an effort to find ways whereby we can fulfill our responsibilities to these thousands of homeless and suffering refugees of all faiths.

INTERNATIONAL TRADE

World economic cooperation is essential to world political cooperation. We have made a good start on economic cooperation through the International Bank, the International Monetary fund, and the Export-Import Bank. We must now take other steps for the reconstruction of world trade and we should continue to strive for an international trade system as free from obstructions as possible.

ATOMIC ENERGY

The United States has taken the lead in the endeavor to put atomic energy under effective international control. We seek no monopoly for ourselves or for any group of nations. We ask only that there be safeguards sufficient to insure that no nation will be able to use this power for military purposes. So long as all governments are not agreed on means of international control of atomic energy, the shadow of fear will obscure the bright prospects for the peaceful use of this enormous power.

In accordance with the Atomic Energy Act of 1946, the Commission established under that law is assuming full jurisdiction over domestic atomic energy enterprise. The program of the Commission will, of course, be worked out in close collaboration with the military services in conformity with the wish of the Congress, but it is my fervent hope that the military significance of atomic energy will steadily decline. We look to the Commission to foster the development of atomic energy for industrial use and scientific and medical research. In the vigorous and effective development of peaceful uses of atomic energy rests our hope that this new force may ultimately be turned into a blessing for all nations.

MILITARY POLICY

In 1946 the Army and Navy completed the demobilization of their wartime forces. They are now maintaining the forces which we need for national defense and to fulfill our international obligations.

We live in a world in which strength on the part of peace-loving nations is still the greatest deterrent to aggression. World stability can be destroyed when nations with great responsibilities neglect to maintain the means of discharging those responsibilities.

This is an age when unforeseen attack could come with unprecedented speed. We must be strong enough to defeat, and thus forestall, any such attack. In our steady Progress toward a more rational world order, the need for large armed forces is progressively declining; but the stabilizing force of American military strength must not be weakened until our hopes are fully realized. When a system of collective security under the United Nations has been established, we shall be willing to lead in collective disarmament, but, until such a system becomes a reality, we must not again allow ourselves to become weak and invite attack.

For those reasons, we need well-equipped, well-trained armed forces and we must be able to mobilize rapidly our resources in men and material for our own defense, should the need arise.

The Army will be reduced to 1,070,000 officers and men by July 1, 1947. Half of the Army will be used for occupation duties abroad and most of the remainder will be employed at home in the support of these overseas forces.

The Navy is supporting the occupation troops in Europe and in the Far East. Its fundamental mission—to support our national interests wherever required—is unchanged. The Navy, including the Marine Corps, will average 571,000 officers and men during the fiscal year 1948.

We are encountering serious difficulties in maintaining our forces at even these reduced levels. Occupation troops are barely sufficient to carry out the duties which our foreign policy requires. Our forces at home are at a point where further reduction is impracticable. We should like an Army and a Navy composed entirely of long-term volunteers, but in spite of liberal inducements the basic needs of the Army are not now being met by voluntary enlistments.

The War Department has advised me that it is unable to

make an accurate forecast at the present time as to whether it will be possible to maintain the strength of the Army by relying exclusively on volunteers. The situation will be much clearer in a few weeks, when the results of the campaign for volunteers are known. The War Department will make its recommendations as to the need for the extension of Selective Service in sufficient time to enable the Congress to take action prior to the expiration of the present law on March 31st. The responsibility for maintaining our armed forces at the strength necessary for our national safety rests with the Congress.

The development of a trained citizen reserve is also vital to our national security. This can best be accomplished through universal training. I have appointed an Advisory Commission on Universal Training to study the various plans for a training program, and I expect that the recommendations of the Commission will be of benefit to the Congress and to me in reaching decisions on this problem.

The cost of the military establishment is substantial. There is one certain way by which we can cut costs and at the same time enhance our national security. That is by the establishment of a single Department of National Defense. I shall communicate with the Congress in the near future with reference to the establishment of a single Department of National Defense.

National security does not consist only of an army, a navy, and an air force. It rests on a much broader basis. It depends on a sound economy of prices and wages, on prosperous agriculture, on satisfied and productive workers, on a competitive private enterprise free from monopolistic repression, on continued industrial harmony and production, on civil liberties and human freedoms-on all the forces which create in our men and women a strong moral fiber and spiritual stamina.

But we have a higher duty and a greater responsibility than the attainment of our own national security. Our goal is collective security for all mankind.

If we can work in a spirit of understanding and mutual respect, we can fulfill this solemn obligation which rests upon us.

The spirit of the American people can set the course of world history. If we maintain and strengthen our cherished ideals, and if we share our great bounty with war-stricken people over the world, then the faith of our citizens in freedom and democracy will be spread over the whole earth and free men everywhere will share our devotion to those ideals.

Let us have the will and the patience to this job together.

May the Lord strengthen us in our faith.

May He give us wisdom to lead the peoples of the world in His ways of peace.

State of the Union Address Harry S. Truman

January 7, 1948

Mr. President, Mr. Speaker, and Members of the 80th Congress:

We are here today to consider the state of the Union.

On this occasion, above all others, the Congress and the President should concentrate their attention, not upon party but upon the country; not upon things which divide us but upon those which bind us together—the enduring principles of our American system, and our common aspirations for the future welfare and security of the people of the United States.

The United States has become great because [p.2] we, as a people, have been able to work together for great objectives even while differing about details.

The elements of our strength are many. They include our democratic government, our economic system, our great natural resources. But these are only partial explanations.

The basic source of our strength is spiritual. For we are a people with a faith. We believe in the dignity of man. We believe that he was created in the image of the Father of us all.

We do not believe that men exist merely to strengthen the state or to be cogs in the economic machine. We do believe that governments are created to serve the people and that economic systems exist to minister to their wants. We have a profound devotion to the welfare and rights of the individual as a human being.

The faith of our people has particular meaning at this time in history because of the unsettled and changing state of the world.

The victims of war in many lands are striving to rebuild their lives, and are seeking assurance that the tragedy of war will not occur again. Throughout the world new ideas are challenging the old. Men of all nations are reexamining the beliefs by which they live. Great scientific and industrial changes have released new forces which will affect the future course of civilization.

The state of our Union reflects the changing nature of the modern world. On all sides there is heartening evidence of great energy—of capacity for economic development-and even more important, capacity for spiritual growth. But accompanying this great activity there are equally great questions, great anxieties, and great aspirations. They represent the concern of an enlightened people that conditions should be so arranged as to make life more worthwhile.

We must devote ourselves to finding answers to these anxieties and aspirations. We seek answers which will embody the moral and spiritual elements of tolerance, unselfishness, and brotherhood upon which true freedom and opportunity must rest.

As we examine the state of our Union today, we can benefit from viewing it on a basis of the accomplishments of the last decade and of our goals for the next. How far have we come during the last 10 years and how far can we go in the next 10?

It was 10 years ago that the determination of dictators to wage war upon mankind became apparent. The years that followed brought untold death and destruction.

We shared in the human suffering of the war, but we were fortunate enough to escape most of war's destruction. We were able through these 10 years to expand the productive strength of our farms and factories.

More important, however, is the fact that these years brought us new courage, new confidence in the ideals of our free democracy. Our deep belief in freedom and justice was reinforced in the crucible of war.

On the foundations of our greatly strengthened economy and our renewed confidence in democratic values, we can continue to move forward.

There are some who look with fear and distrust upon planning for the future. Yet our great national achievements have been attained by those with vision. Our Union was formed, our frontiers were pushed back, and our great industries were built by men who looked ahead.

I propose that we look ahead today toward those goals for the future which have the greatest bearing upon the foundations of our democracy and the happiness of our people.

I do so, confident in the thought that with clear objectives and with firm determination, we can, in the next 10 years, build upon the [p.3] accomplishments of the past decade to achieve a glorious future. Year by year, beginning now, we must make a substantial part of this progress.

Our first goal is to secure fully the essential human rights of our citizens.

The United States has always had a deep concern for human rights. Religious freedom, free speech, and freedom of thought are cherished realities in our land. Any denial of human rights is a denial of the basic beliefs of democracy and of our regard for the worth of each individual.

Today, however, some of our citizens are still denied equal opportunity for education, for jobs and economic advancement, and for the expression of their views at the polls. Most serious of all, some are denied equal protection under laws. Whether discrimination is based on race, or creed, or color, or land of origin, it is utterly contrary to American ideals of democracy.

The recent report of the President's Committee on Civil Rights points the way to corrective action by the Federal Government and by State and local governments. Because of the need for effective Federal action, I shall send a special message to the Congress on this important subject.

We should also consider our obligation to assure the fullest possible measure of civil rights to the people of our territories and possessions. I believe that the time has come for Alaska and Hawaii to be admitted to the Union as States.

Our second goal is to protect and develop our human resources.

The safeguarding of the rights of our citizens must be accompanied by an equal regard for their opportunities for development and their protection from economic insecurity. In this Nation the ideals of freedom and equality can be given specific meaning in terms of health, education, social security, and housing.

Over the past 12 years we have erected a sound framework of social security legislation. Many millions of our citizens are now protected against the loss of income which can come with unemployment, old age, or the death of wage earners. Yet our system has gaps and inconsistencies; it is only half finished.

We should now extend unemployment compensation, old age benefits, and survivors' benefits to millions who are not now protected. We should also raise the level of benefits.

The greatest gap in our social security structure is the lack of adequate provision for the Nation's health. We are rightly proud of the high standards of medical care we know how to provide in the United States. The fact is, however, that most of our people cannot afford to pay for the care they need.

I have often and strongly urged that this condition demands a national health program. The heart of the program must be a national system of payment for medical care based on well-tried insurance principles. This great Nation cannot afford to allow its citizens to suffer needlessly from the lack of proper medical care.

Our ultimate aim must be a comprehensive insurance system to protect all our people equally against insecurity and ill health.

Another fundamental aim of our democracy is to provide an adequate education for every person.

Our educational systems face a financial crisis. It is deplorable that in a Nation as rich as ours there are millions of children who do not have adequate schoolhouses or enough teachers for a good elementary or secondary education. If there are educational inadequacies in any State, the whole Nation suffers. The Federal Government has a responsibility for providing financial aid to meet this crisis.

In addition, we must make possible greater equality of opportunity to all our citizens for education. Only by so doing can we insure that our citizens will be capable of understanding and sharing the responsibilities of democracy.

The Government's programs for health, education, and security are of such great importance to our democracy that we should now establish an executive department for their administration.

Health and education have their beginning in the home. No matter what our hospitals or schools are like, the youth of our Nation are handicapped when millions of them live in city slums and country shacks. Within the next decade, we must see that every American family has a decent home. As an immediate step we need the long-range housing program which I have recommended on many occasions to this

Congress. This should include financial aids designed to yield more housing at lower prices. It should provide public housing for low-income families, and vigorous development of new techniques to lower the cost of building.

Until we can overcome the present drastic housing shortage, we must extend and strengthen rent control.

We have had, and shall continue to have, a special interest in the welfare of our veterans. Over 14 million men and women who served in the armed forces in World War II have now returned to civilian life. Over 2 million veterans are being helped through school. Millions have been aided while finding jobs, and have been helped in buying homes, in obtaining medical care, and in adjusting themselves to physical handicaps.

All but a very few veterans have successfully made the transition from military life to their home communities. The success of our veterans' program is proved by this fact. This Nation is proud of the eagerness shown by our veterans to become self-reliant and self-supporting citizens.

Our third goal is to conserve and use our natural resources so that they can contribute most effectively to the welfare of our people.

The resources given by nature to this country are rich and extensive. The material foundations of our growth and economic development are the bounty of our fields, the wealth of our mines and forests, and the energy of our waters. As a Nation, we are coming to appreciate more each day the dose relationship between the conservation of these resources and the preservation of our national strength.

We are doing far less than we know how to do to make use

of our resources without destroying them. Both the public and private use of these resources must have the primary objective of maintaining and increasing these basic supports for an expanding future.

We must continue to take specific steps toward this goal. We must vigorously defend our natural wealth against those who would misuse it for selfish gain.

We need accurate and comprehensive knowledge of our mineral resources and must intensify our efforts to develop new supplies and to acquire stockpiles of scarce materials.

We need to protect and restore our land-public and private—through combating erosion and rebuilding the fertility of the soil.

We must expand our reclamation program to bring millions of acres of arid land into production, and to improve water supplies for additional millions of acres. This will provide new opportunities for veterans and others, particularly in the West, and aid in providing a rising living standard for a growing population.

We must protect and restore our forests by sustained-yield forestry and by planting [p.5] new trees in areas now slashed and barren.

We must continue to erect multiple-purpose dams on our great rivers—not only to reclaim land, but also to prevent floods, to extend our inland waterways and to provide hydroelectric power. This public power must not be monopolized for private gain. Only through well-established policies of transmitting power directly to its market and thus encouraging widespread use at low rates can the Federal Government assure the people of their full share of its benefits. Additional power—public and private—is needed to raise the ceilings now imposed by power shortages on industrial and agricultural development.

We should achieve the wise use of resources through the integrated development of our great river basins. We can learn much from our Tennessee Valley experience. We should no longer delay in applying the lessons of that vast undertaking to our other great river basins.

Our fourth goal is to lift the standard of living for all our people by strengthening our economic system and sharing more broadly among our people the goods we produce.

The amazing economic progress of the past 10 years points the way for the next 10.

Today 14 million more people have jobs than in 1938.

Our yearly output of goods and services has increased by two-thirds.

The average income of our people, measured in dollars of equal purchasing power, has increased—after taxes—by more than 50 percent.

In no other 10 years have farmers, businessmen, and wage earners made such great gains.

We may not be able to expand as rapidly in the next decade as in the last, because we are now starting from full employment and very high production. But we can increase our annual output by at least one-third above the present level. We can lift our standard of living to nearly double what it was 10 years ago.

If we distribute these gains properly, we can go far toward stamping out poverty in our generation.

To do this, agriculture, business, and labor must move forward together.

Permanent farm prosperity and agricultural abundance will be achieved only as our whole economy grows and prospers. The farmer can sell more food at good prices when the incomes of wage earners are high and when there is full employment. Adequate diets for every American family, and the needs of our industries at full production, will absorb a farm output well above our present levels.

Although the average farmer is now better off than ever before, farm families as a whole have only begun to catch up with the standards of living enjoyed in the cities. In 1946, the average income of farm people was $779, contrasted with an average income of $1,288 for nonfarm people. Within the next decade, we should eliminate elements of inequality in these living standards.

To this end our farm program should enable the farmer to market his varied crops at fair price levels and to improve his standard of living.

We need to continue price supports for major farm commodities on a basis which will afford reasonable protection against fluctuations in the levels of production and demand. The present price support program must be reexamined and modernized.

Crop insurance should be strengthened and its benefits extended in order to protect the farmer against the special hazards to which he is subject.

We also need to improve the means for getting farm products into markets and into the hands of consumers. Cooperatives which [p.6] directly or indirectly serve this purpose must be encouraged—not discouraged. The school lunch program should be continued and adequately financed.

We need to go forward with the rural electrification program to bring the benefits of electricity to all our farm population.

We can, and must, aid and encourage farmers to conserve their soil resources and restore the fertility of the land that has suffered from neglect or unwise use.

All these are practical measures upon which we should act immediately to enable agriculture to make its full contribution to our prosperity.

We must also strengthen our economic system within the next decade by enlarging our industrial capacity within the framework of our free enterprise system.

We are today far short of the industrial capacity we need for a growing future. At least $50 billion should be invested by industry to improve and expand our productive facilities over the next few years. But this is only the beginning. The industrial application of atomic energy and other scientific advances will constantly open up further opportunities for expansion. Farm prosperity and high employment will call for an immensely increased output of goods and services.

Growth and vitality in our economy depend on vigorous private enterprise. Free competition is the key to industrial development, full production and employment, fair prices, and an ever improving standard of living. Competition is seriously limited today in many industries by the concentration of economic power and other elements of monopoly. The appropriation of sufficient funds to permit proper enforcement of the present antitrust laws is essential. Beyond that we should go on to strengthen our legislation to protect competition.

Another basic element of a strong economic system is the well-being of the wage earners.

We have learned that the well-being of workers depends on high production and consequent high employment. We have learned equally well that the welfare of industry and agriculture depends on high incomes for our workers.

The Government has wisely chosen to set a floor under wages. But our 40-cent minimum wage is inadequate and obsolete. I recommend the lifting of the minimum wage to 75 cents an hour.

In general, however, we must continue to rely on our sound system of collective bargaining to set wage scales. Workers' incomes should increase at a rate consistent with the maintenance of sound price, profit, and wage relationships and with increase of productivity.

The Government's part in labor-management relations is now largely controlled by the terms of the Labor-Management Relations Act of 1947. I made my attitude clear on this act in my veto message to the Congress last June. Nothing has occurred since to change my opinion of this law. As long as it remains the law of the land, however, I shall carry out my constitutional duty and administer it.

As we look ahead we can understand the crucial importance of restraint and wisdom in arriving at new labor-management contracts. Work stoppages would result in a loss of production—a loss which could bring higher prices for our citizens and could also deny the necessities of life to the hard-pressed peoples of other lands. It is my sincere hope that the representatives of labor and of industry will bear in mind that the Nation as a whole has a vital stake in the success of their bargaining efforts.

If we surmount our current economic difficulties, we can move ahead to a great increase [p.7] in our national income which will enable all our people to enjoy richer and fuller lives.

All of us must advance together. One-fifth of our families now have average annual incomes of less than $850. We must see that our gains in national income are made more largely available to those with low incomes, whose need is greatest. This will benefit us all through providing a stable foundation of buying power to maintain prosperity.

Business, labor, agriculture, and Government, working together, must develop the policies which will make possible the realization of the full benefits of our economic system.

Our fifth goal is to achieve world peace based on principles of freedom and justice and the equality of all nations.

Twice within our generation, world wars have taught us that we cannot isolate ourselves from the rest of the world.

We have learned that the loss of freedom in any area of the world means a loss of freedom to ourselves—that the loss of independence by any nation adds directly to the insecurity of the United States and all free nations.

We have learned that a healthy world economy is essential to world peace—that economic distress is a disease whose evil effects spread far beyond the boundaries of the afflicted nation.

For these reasons the United States is vigorously following policies designed to achieve a peaceful and prosperous world.

We are giving, and will continue to give, our full support to the United Nations. While that organization has encountered unforeseen and unwelcome difficulties, I am confident of its ultimate success. We are also devoting our efforts toward world economic recovery and the revival of world trade. These actions are closely related and mutually supporting.

We believe that the United States can be an effective force for world peace only if it is strong. We look forward to the day when nations will decrease their armaments. Yet so long as there remains serious opposition to the ideals of a peaceful world, we must maintain strong armed forces.

The passage of the National Security Act by the Congress at its last session was a notable step in providing for the security of this country. A further step which I consider of even greater importance is the early provision for universal training. There are many elements in a balanced national security program, all interrelated and necessary, but universal training should be the foundation for them all. A favorable decision by the Congress at an early date is of world importance. I am convinced that such action is vital to the security of this Nation and to the maintenance of its leadership.

The United States is engaged today in many international activities directed toward the creation of lasting peaceful relationships among nations.

We have been giving substantial aid to Greece and Turkey to assist those nations in preserving their integrity against foreign pressures. Had it not been for our aid, their situation today might well be radically different. The continued integrity of those countries will have a powerful effect upon other nations in the Middle East and in Europe struggling to maintain their independence while they repair the damages of war.

The United States has special responsibilities with respect to the countries in which we have occupation forces: Germany, Austria, Japan, and Korea. Our efforts to reach agreements on peace settlements for these countries have so far been blocked. But we [p.8] shall continue to exert our utmost efforts to obtain satisfactory settlements for each of these nations.

Many thousands of displaced persons, still living in camps overseas, should be allowed entry into the United States. I again urge the Congress to pass suitable legislation at once so that this Nation may do its share in caring for the homeless and suffering refugees of all faiths. I believe that the admission of these persons will add to the strength and energy of this Nation.

We are moving toward our goal of world peace in many ways. But the most important efforts which we are now making are those which support world economic reconstruction. We are seeking to restore the world trading system which was shattered by the war and to remedy the economic paralysis which grips many countries.

To restore world trade we have recently taken the lead in bringing about the greatest reduction of world tariffs that the world has ever seen. The extension of the provisions of the Reciprocal Trade Agreements Act, which made this achievement possible, is of extreme importance. We must also go on to support the International Trade Organization, through which we hope to obtain worldwide agreement on a code of fair conduct in international trade.

Our present major effort toward economic reconstruction is to support the program for recovery developed by the countries of Europe. In my recent message to the Congress, I outlined the reasons why it is wise and necessary for the United States to extend this support.

I want to reaffirm my belief in the soundness and the promise of this proposal. When the European economy is strengthened, the product of its industry will be of benefit to many other areas of economic distress. The ability of free men to overcome hunger and despair will be a moral stimulus to the entire world.

We intend to work also with other nations in achieving world economic recovery. We shall continue our cooperation with the nations of the Western Hemisphere. A special program of assistance to China, to provide urgent relief needs and to speed reconstruction, will be submitted to the Congress.

Unfortunately, not all governments share the hope of the people of the United States that economic reconstruction in many areas of the world can be achieved through cooperative effort among nations. In spite of these differences we will go forward with our efforts to overcome economic paralysis.

No nation by itself can carry these programs to success; they depend upon the cooperative and honest efforts of all participating countries. Yet the leadership is inevitably ours.

I consider it of the highest importance that the Congress should authorize support for the European recovery program for the period from April 1, 1948, to June 30, 1952, with an initial amount for the first 15 months of $6.8 billion. I urge the Congress to act promptly on this vital measure of our foreign policy—on this decisive contribution to world peace.

We are following a sound, constructive, and practical course in carrying out our determination to achieve peace.

We are fighting poverty, hunger, and suffering.

This leads to peace—not war.

We are building toward a world where all nations, large and small alike, may live

free from the fear of aggression. This leads to peace—not war.

Above all else, we are striving to achieve a concord among the peoples of the world based upon the dignity of the individual and the brotherhood of man.

This leads to peace—not war.

We can go forward with confidence that we are following sound policies, both at home and with other nations, which will lead us toward our great goals for economic, social and moral achievement.

As we enter the new year, we must surmount one major problem which affects all our goals. That is the problem of inflation.

Already inflation in this country is undermining the living standards of millions of families. Food costs too much. Housing has reached fantastic price levels. Schools and hospitals are in financial distress. Inflation threatens to bring on disagreement and strife between labor and management.

Worst of all, inflation holds the threat of another depression, just as we had a depression after the unstable boom following the First World War.

When I announced last October that the Congress was being called into session, I described the price increases which had taken place since June 1946. Wholesale prices had increased 40 percent; retail prices had increased 23 percent.

Since October prices have continued to rise. Wholesale prices have gone up at an annual rate of 18 percent. Retail prices have gone up at an annual rate of 10 percent.

The events which have occurred since I presented my 10-point anti-inflation program to the Congress in November have made it even clearer that all 10 points are essential.

High prices must not be our means of rationing.

We must deal effectively and at once with the high cost of living.

We must stop the spiral of inflation.

I trust that within the shortest possible time the Congress will make available to the Government the weapons that are so desperately needed in the fight against inflation.

One of the most powerful anti-inflationary factors in our economy today is the excess of Government revenues over expenditures.

Government expenditures have been and must continue to be held at the lowest safe levels. Since V-J day Federal expenditures have been sharply reduced. They have been cut from more than $63 billion in the fiscal year 1946 to less than $38 billion in the present fiscal year. The number of civilian employees has been cut nearly in half—from 3 3/4 million down to 2 million.

On the other hand, Government revenues must not be reduced. Until inflation has been stopped there should be no cut in taxes that is not offset by additions at another point in our tax structure.

Certain adjustments should be made within our existing tax structure that will not affect total receipts, yet will adjust the tax burden so that those least able to pay will have their burden lessened by the transfer of a portion of it to those best able to pay.

Many of our families today are suffering hardship because of the high cost of living. At the same time profits of corporations have reached an all-time record in 1947. Corporate profits total $17 billion after taxes. This compared with $12.5 billion in 1946, the previous high year.

Because of this extraordinarily high level of profits, corporations can well afford to carry a larger share of the taxload at this time.

During this period in which the high cost of living is bearing down on so many of our families, tax adjustments should be made to ease their burden. The low-income group particularly is being pressed very hard. To this group a tax adjustment would result in a saving that could be used to buy the necessities of life.

I recommend therefore that, effective January 1, 1948, a cost of living tax credit be extended to our people consisting of a credit of $40 to each individual taxpayer and an additional credit of $40 for each dependent. [p.10] Thus the income tax of a man with a wife and two children would be reduced $160. The credit would be extended to all taxpayers, but it would be particularly helpful to those in the low-income group.

It is estimated that such a tax credit would reduce Federal revenue by $3.2 billion. This reduction should be made up by increasing the tax on corporate profits in an amount that will produce this sum—with appropriate adjustments for small corporations.

This is the proper method of tax relief at this time. It gives relief to those who need it most without cutting the total tax revenue of the Government.

When the present danger of inflation has passed we should consider tax reduction based upon a revision of our entire tax structure.

When we have conquered inflation, we shall be in a position to move forward toward our chosen goals.

As we do so, let us keep ever before us our high purposes. We are determined that every citizen of this Nation shall have an equal right and an equal opportunity to grow in wisdom and in stature and to take his place in the control of his Nation's destiny.

We are determined that the productive resources of this Nation shall be used wisely and fully for the benefit of all.

We are determined that the democratic faith of our people and the strength of our resources shall contribute their full share to the attainment of enduring peace in the world.

It is our faith in human dignity that underlies these purposes. It is this faith that keeps us a strong and vital people.

This is a time to remind ourselves of these fundamentals. For today the whole world looks to us for leadership.

This is the hour to rededicate ourselves to the faith in mankind that makes us strong.

This is the hour to rededicate ourselves to the faith in God that gives us confidence as we face the challenge of the years ahead.

State of the Union Address Harry S. Truman

January 5, 1949

Mr. President, Mr. Speaker, Members of the Congress:

I am happy to report to this 81st Congress that the state of the Union is good. Our Nation is better able than ever before to meet the needs of the American people, and to give them their fair chance in the pursuit of happiness. This great Republic is foremost among the nations of the world in the search for peace.

During the last 16 years, our people have been creating a society which offers new opportunities for every man to enjoy his share of the good things of life.

In this society, we are conservative about the values and principles which we cherish; but we are forward-looking in protecting those values and principles and in extending their benefits. We have rejected the discredited theory that the fortunes of the Nation should be in the hands of a privileged few. We have abandoned the "trickledown" concept of national prosperity. Instead, we believe that our economic system should rest on a democratic foundation and that wealth should be created for the benefit of all.

The recent election shows that the people of the United States are in favor of this kind of society and want to go on improving it.

The American people have decided that poverty is just as wasteful and just as unnecessary as preventable disease. We have pledged our common resources to help one another in the hazards and struggles of individual life. We believe that no unfair prejudice or artificial distinction should bar any citizen of the United States of America from an education, or from good health, or from a job that he is capable of performing.

The attainment of this kind of society demands the best efforts of every citizen in every walk of life, and it imposes increasing responsibilities on the Government.

The Government must work with industry, labor, and the farmers in keeping our economy running at full speed. The Government must see that every American has a chance to obtain his fair share of our increasing abundance. These responsibilities go hand in hand.

We cannot maintain prosperity unless we have a fair distribution of opportunity and a widespread consumption of the products of our factories and farms.

Our Government has undertaken to meet these responsibilities.

We have ,made tremendous public investments in highways, hydroelectric power projects, soil conservation, and reclamation. We have established a system of social security. We have enacted laws protecting the rights and the welfare of our working people and the income of our farmers. These Federal policies have paid for themselves many times over. They have strengthened the material foundations of our democratic ideals. Without them, our present prosperity would be impossible.

Reinforced by these policies, our private enterprise system has reached new heights of production. Since the boom year of 1929, while our population has increased by only 20 percent, our agricultural production has increased by 45 percent, and our industrial production has increased by 75 percent. We are turning out far more goods and more wealth per worker than we have ever done before.

This progress has confounded the gloomy prophets—at home and abroad who predicted the downfall of American capitalism. The people of the United States, going their own way, confident in their own powers, have achieved the greatest prosperity the world has even seen.

But, great as our progress has been, we still have a long way to go.

As we look around the country, many of our shortcomings stand out in bold relief.

We are suffering from excessively high prices.

Our production is still not large enough to satisfy our demands.

Our minimum wages are far too low.

Small business is losing ground to growing monopoly.

Our farmers still face an uncertain future. And too many of them lack the benefits of our modern civilization.

Some of our natural resources are still being wasted.

We are acutely short of electric power, although the means for developing such power are abundant.

Five million families are still living in slums and firetraps. Three million families share their homes with others.

Our health is far behind the progress of medical science. Proper medical care is so expensive that it is out of the reach of the great majority of our citizens.

Our schools, in many localities, are utterly inadequate.

Our democratic ideals are often thwarted by prejudice and intolerance.

Each of these shortcomings is also an opportunity-an opportunity for the Congress and the President to work for the good of the people.

Our first great opportunity is to protect our economy against the evils of "boom and bust."

This objective cannot be attained by government alone. Indeed, the greater part of the task must be performed by individual efforts under our system of free enterprise. We can keep our present prosperity, and increase it, only if free enterprise and free government work together to that end.

We cannot afford to float along ceaselessly on a postwar boom until it collapses. It is not enough merely to prepare to weather a recession if it comes. Instead, government and business must work together constantly to achieve more and more jobs and more and more production—which mean more and more prosperity for all the people.

The business cycle is man-made; and men of good will, working together, can smooth it out.

So far as business is concerned, it should plan for steady, vigorous expansion—seeking always to increase its output, lower its prices, and avoid the vices of monopoly and restriction. So long as business does this, it will be contributing to continued prosperity, and it will have the help and encouragement of the Government.

The Employment Act of 1946 pledges the Government to use all its resources to promote maximum employment, production, and purchasing power. This means that the Government is firmly committed to protect business and the people against the dangers of recession and against the evils of inflation. This means that the Government must adapt its plans and policies to meet changing circumstances.

At the present time, our prosperity is threatened by inflationary pressures at a number of critical points in our economy. And the Government must be in a position to take effective action at these danger spots. To that end, I recommend that the Congress enact legislation for the following purposes:

First, to continue the power to control consumer credit and enlarge the power to control bank credit.

Second, to grant authority to regulate speculation on the commodity exchanges.

Third, to continue export control authority and to provide adequate machinery for its enforcement.

Fourth, to continue the priorities and allocation authority in the field of transportation.

Fifth, to authorize priorities and allocations for key materials in short supply.

Sixth, to extend and strengthen rent control.

Seventh, to provide standby authority to impose price ceilings for scarce commodities which basically affect essential industrial production or the cost of living, and to limit unjustified wage adjustments which would force a break in an established price ceiling.

Eighth, to authorize an immediate study of the adequacy of production facilities for materials in critically short supply, such as steel; and, if found necessary, to authorize Government loans for the expansion of production facilities to relieve such shortages, and to authorize the construction of such facilities directly, if action by private industry fails to meet our needs.

The Economic Report, which I shall submit to the Congress shortly, will discuss in detail the economic background for these recommendations.

One of the most important factors in maintaining prosperity is the Government's fiscal policy. At this time, it is essential not only that the Federal budget be balanced, but also that there be a substantial surplus to reduce inflationary pressures, and to permit a sizable reduction in the national debt, which now stands at $252 billion. I recommend, therefore, that the Congress enact new tax legislation to bring in an additional $4 billion of Government revenue. This should come principally from additional corporate taxes. A portion should come from revised estate and gift taxes. Consideration should be given to raising personal income rates in the middle and upper brackets.

If we want to keep our economy running in high gear, we must be sure that every group has the incentive to make its full contribution to the national welfare. At present, the working men and women of the Nation are unfairly discriminated against by a statute that abridges their rights, curtails their constructive efforts, and hampers our system of free collective bargaining. That statute is the Labor-Management Relations Act of 1947, sometimes called the Taft-Hartley Act.

That act should be repealed!

The Wagner Act should be reenacted. However, certain improvements, which I recommended to the Congress 2 years ago, are needed. Jurisdictional strikes and unjustified secondary boycotts should be prohibited. The use of economic force to decide issues arising out of the interpretation of existing contracts should be prevented. Without endangering our democratic freedoms, means should be provided for setting up machinery for preventing strikes in vital industries which affect the public interest.

The Department of Labor should be rebuilt and strengthened and those units properly belonging within that department should be placed in it.

The health of our economy and its maintenance at high levels further require that the minimum wage fixed by law should be raised to at least 75 cents an hour.

If our free enterprise economy is to be strong and healthy, we must reinvigorate the forces of competition. We must assure small business the freedom and opportunity to grow and prosper. To this purpose, we should strengthen our antitrust laws by closing those loopholes that permit monopolistic mergers and consolidations.

Our national farm program should be improved-not only in the interest of the farmers, but for the lasting prosperity of the whole Nation. Our goals should be abundant farm production and parity income for agriculture. Standards of living on the farm should be just as good as anywhere else in the country.

Farm price supports are an essential part of our program to achieve these ends. Price supports should be used to prevent farm price declines which are out of line with general price levels, to facilitate adjustments in production to consumer demands, and to promote good land use. Our price support legislation must be adapted to these objectives. The authority of the Commodity Credit Corporation to provide adequate storage space for crops should be restored.

Our program for farm prosperity should also seek to expand the domestic market for agricultural products, particularly among low-income groups, and to increase and stabilize foreign markets.

We should give special attention to extending modern conveniences and services to our farms. Rural electrification should be pushed forward. And in considering legislation relating to housing, education, health, and social security, special attention should be given to rural problems.

Our growing population and the expansion of our economy depend upon the wise management of our land, water, forest, and mineral wealth. In our present dynamic economy, the task of conservation is not to lockup our resources but to develop and improve them. Failure, today, to make the investments which are necessary to support our progress in the future would be false economy.

We must push forward the development of our rivers for power, irrigation, navigation, and flood control. We should apply the lessons of our Tennessee Valley experience to our other great river basins.

I again recommend action be taken by the Congress to approve the St. Lawrence Seaway and Power project. This is about the fifth time I have recommended it.

We must adopt a program for the planned use of the petroleum reserves under the sea, which are—and must remain—vested in the Federal Government. We must extend our programs of soil conservation. We must place our forests on a sustained yield basis, and encourage the development of new sources of vital minerals.

In all this we must make sure that the benefits of these public undertakings are directly available to the people. Public power should be carried to consuming areas by public transmission lines where necessary to provide electricity at the lowest possible rates. Irrigation waters should serve family farms and not land speculators.

The Government has still other opportunities—to help raise the standard of living of our citizens. These opportunities lie in the fields of social security, health, education, housing, and civil rights.

The present coverage of the social security laws is altogether inadequate; the benefit payments are too low. One-third of our workers are not covered. Those who receive old-age and survivors insurance benefits receive an average payment of only $25 a month. Many others who cannot work because they are physically disabled are left to the mercy of charity. We should expand our social security program, both as to the size of the benefits and the extent of coverage, against the economic hazards due to unemployment, old age, sickness, and disability.

We must spare no effort to raise the general level of health in this country. In a nation as rich as ours, it is a shocking fact that tens of millions lack adequate medical care. We are short of doctors, hospitals, nurses. We must remedy these shortages. Moreover, we need—and we must have without further delay—a system of prepaid medical insurance which will enable every American to afford good medical care.

It is equally shocking that millions of our children are not receiving a good education. Millions of them are in overcrowded, obsolete buildings. We are short of teachers, because teachers' salaries are too low to attract new teachers, or to hold the ones we have. All these school problems will become much more acute as a result of the tremendous increase in the enrollment in our elementary schools in the next few years. I cannot repeat too strongly my desire for prompt Federal financial aid to the States to help them operate and maintain their school systems.

The governmental agency which now administers the programs of health, education, and social security should be given full departmental status.

The housing shortage continues to be acute. As an immediate step, the Congress should enact the provisions for low-rent public housing, slum clearance, farm housing, and housing research which I have repeatedly recommended. The number of lowrent public housing units provided for in the legislation should be increased to 1 million units in the next 7 years. Even this number of units will not begin to meet our need for new housing.

Most of the houses we need will have to be built by private enterprise, without public subsidy. By producing too few rental units and too large a proportion of high-priced houses, the building industry is rapidly pricing itself out of the market. Building costs must be lowered.

The Government is now engaged in a campaign to induce all segments of the building industry to concentrate on the production of lower priced housing. Additional legislation to encourage such housing will be submitted.

The authority which I have requested, to allocate materials in short supply and to impose price ceilings on such materials, could be used, if found necessary, to channel more materials into homes large enough for family life at prices which wage earners can afford.

The driving force behind our progress is our faith in our democratic institutions. That faith is embodied in the promise of equal rights and equal opportunities which the founders of our Republic proclaimed to their countrymen and to the whole world.

The fulfillment of this promise is among the highest purposes of government. The civil rights proposals I made to the 80th Congress, I now repeat to the 81st Congress. They should be enacted in order that the Federal Government may assume the leadership and discharge the obligations dearly placed upon it by the Constitution.

I stand squarely behind those proposals.

Our domestic programs are the foundation of our foreign policy. The world today looks to us for leadership because we have so largely realized, within our borders, those benefits of democratic government for which most of the peoples of the world are yearning.

We are following a foreign policy which is the outward expression of the democratic faith we profess. We are doing what we can to encourage free states and free peoples throughout the world, to aid the suffering and afflicted in foreign lands, and to strengthen democratic nations against aggression.

The heart of our foreign policy is peace. We are supporting a world organization to keep peace and a world economic policy to create prosperity for mankind. Our guiding star is the principle of international cooperation. To this concept we have made a national commitment as profound as anything in history.

To it we have pledged our resources and our honor.

Until a system of world security is established upon which we can safely rely, we cannot escape the burden of creating and maintaining armed forces sufficient to deter aggression. We have made great progress in the last year in the effective organization of our Armed Forces, but further improvements in our national security legislation are necessary. Universal training is essential to the security of the United States.

During the course of this session I shall have occasion to ask the Congress to consider several measures in the field of foreign policy. At this time, I recommend that we restore the Reciprocal Trade Agreements Act to full effectiveness, and extend it for 3 years. We should also open our doors to displaced persons without unfair discrimination.

It should be clear by now to all citizens that we are not

seeking to freeze the status quo. We have no intention of preserving the injustices of the past. We welcome the constructive efforts being made by many nations to achieve a better life for their citizens. In the European recovery program, in our good-neighbor policy and in the United Nations, we have begun to batter down those national walls which block the economic growth and the social advancement of the peoples of the world.

We believe that if we hold resolutely to this course, the principle of international cooperation will eventually command the approval even of those nations which are now seeking to weaken or subvert it.

We stand at the opening of an era which can mean either great achievement or terrible catastrophe for ourselves and for all mankind.

The strength of our Nation must continue to be used in the interest of all our people rather than a privileged few. It must continue to be used unselfishly in the struggle for world peace and the betterment of mankind the world over.

This is the task before us.

It is not an easy one. It has many complications, and there will be strong opposition from selfish interests.

I hope for cooperation from farmers, from labor, and from business. Every segment of our population and every individual has a right to expect from our Government a fair deal.

In 1945, when I came down before the Congress for the first time on April 16, I quoted to you King Solomon's prayer that he wanted wisdom and the ability to govern his people as they should be governed. I explained to you at that time that the task before me was one of the greatest in the history of the world, and that it was necessary to have the complete cooperation of the Congress and the people of the United States.

Well now, we are taking a new start with the same situation. It is absolutely essential that your President have the complete cooperation of the Congress to carry out the great work that must be done to keep the peace in this world, and to keep this country prosperous.

The people of this great country have a right to expect that the Congress and the President will work in closest cooperation with one objective—the welfare of the people of this Nation as a whole.

In the months ahead I know that I shall be able to cooperate with this Congress.

Now, I am confident that the Divine Power which has guided us to this time of fateful responsibility and glorious opportunity will not desert us now.

With that help from Almighty God which we have humbly acknowledged at every turning point in our national life, we shall be able to perform the great tasks which He now sets before us.

State of the Union Address Harry S. Truman

January 4, 1950

Mr. President, Mr. Speaker, Members of the Congress:

A year ago I reported to this Congress that the state of the Union was good. I am happy to be able to report to you today that the state of the Union continues to be good. Our Republic continues to increase in the enjoyment of freedom within its borders, and to offer strength and encouragement to all those who love freedom throughout the world.

During the past year we have made notable progress in strengthening the foundations of peace and freedom, abroad and at home.

We have taken important steps in securing the North Atlantic community against aggression. We have continued our successful support of European recovery. We have returned to our established policy of expanding international trade through reciprocal agreement. We have strengthened our support of the United Nations.

While great problems still confront us, the greatest danger has receded—the possibility which faced us 3 years ago that most of Europe and the Mediterranean area might collapse under totalitarian pressure. Today, the free peoples of the world have new vigor and new hope for the cause of peace.

In our domestic affairs, we have made notable advances toward broader opportunity and a better life for all our citizens.

We have met and reversed the first significant downturn in economic activity since the war. In accomplishing this, Government programs for maintaining employment and purchasing power have been of tremendous benefit. As the result of these programs, and the wisdom and good judgment of our businessmen and workers, major readjustments have been made without widespread suffering.

During the past year, we have also made a good start in providing housing for low-income groups; we have raised minimum wages; we have gone forward with the development of our natural resources; we have given a greater assurance of stability to the farmer; and we have improved the organization and efficiency of our Government.

Today, by the grace of God, we stand a free and prosperous nation with greater possibilities for the future than any people ever had before in the history of the world.

We are now, in this year of 1950, nearing the midpoint of the 20th century.

The first half of this century will be known as the most turbulent and eventful period in recorded history. The swift pace of events promises to make the next 50 years decisive in the history of man on this planet.

The scientific and industrial revolution which began two centuries ago has, in the last 50 years, caught up the peoples of the globe in a common destiny. Two worldshattering wars have proved that no corner of the earth can be isolated from the affairs of mankind.

The human race has reached a turning point. Man has opened the secrets of nature and mastered new powers. If he uses them wisely, he can reach new heights of civilization. If he uses them foolishly, they may destroy him.

Man must create the moral and legal framework for the world which will insure that his new powers are used for good and not for evil. In shaping the outcome, the people of the United States will play a leading role.

Among all the great changes that have occurred in the last 50 years, none is more important than the change in the position of the United States in world affairs. Fifty years ago we were a country devoted largely to our own internal affairs. Our industry was growing, and we had new interests in the Far East and in the Caribbean, but we were primarily concerned with the development of vast areas of our own continental territory.

Today, our population has doubled. Our national production has risen from about $50 billion, in terms of today's prices, to the staggering figure of $255 billion a year. We have a more productive economic system and a greater industrial potential than any other nation on the globe. Our standard of living is an inspiration for all other peoples. Even the slightest changes in our economic and social life have their effect on other countries all around the world.

Our tremendous strength has brought with it tremendous responsibilities. We have moved from the outer edge to the center of world affairs. Other nations look to us for a wise exercise of our economic and military strength, and for vigorous support of the ideals of representative government and a free society. We will not fail them.

Our objective in the world is peace. Our country has joined with others in the task of achieving peace. We know now that this is not an easy task, or a short one. But we are determined to see it through. Both of our great political parties are committed to working together—and I am sure they will continue to work together—to achieve this end. We are prepared to devote our energy and our resources to this task, because we know that our own security and the future of mankind are at stake.

Right here, I want to say that no one appreciates more than I the bipartisan cooperation in foreign affairs which has been enjoyed by this administration.

Our success in working with other nations to achieve peace depends largely on what we do at home. We must preserve our national strength. Strength is not simply a matter of arms and force. It is a matter of economic growth, and social health, and vigorous institutions, public and private. We can achieve peace only if we maintain our productive energy, our democratic institutions, and our firm belief in individual freedom.

Our surest guide in the days that lie ahead will be the spirit in which this great Republic was rounded. We must make our decisions in the conviction that all men are created equal, that they are equally entitled to life, liberty, and the pursuit of happiness, and that the duty of government is to serve these ends.

This country of ours has experienced many blessings, but

none greater than its dedication to these principles. At every point in our history, these ideals have served to correct our failures and shortcomings, to spur us on to greater efforts, and to keep clearly before us the primary purpose of our existence as a nation. They have enshrined for us, a principle of government, the moral imperative to do justice, and the divine command to men to love one another.

These principles give meaning to all that we do.

In foreign policy, they mean that we can never be tolerant of oppression or tyranny. They mean that we must throw our weight on the side of greater freedom and a better life for all peoples. These principles confirm us in carrying out the specific programs for peace which we have already begun.

We shall continue to give our wholehearted support to the United Nations. We believe that this organization can ultimately provide the framework of international law and morality without which mankind cannot survive. It has already set up new standards for the conduct of nations in the Declaration of Human Rights and the Convention on Genocide. It is moving ahead to give meaning to the concept of world brotherhood through a wide variety of cultural, economic, and technical activities.

The events of the past year again showed the value of the United Nations in bringing about the peaceful adjustment of tense international controversies. In Indonesia and in Palestine the efforts of the United Nations have put a stop to bloodshed and paved the way to peaceful settlements.

We are working toward the time when the United Nations will control weapons of mass destruction and will have the forces to preserve international law and order. While the world remains unsettled, however, and as long as our own security and the security of the free world require, we will maintain a strong and well-balanced defense organization. The Selective Service System is an essential part of our defense plans, and it must be continued.

Under the principles of the United Nations Charter we must continue to share in the common defense of free nations against aggression. At the last session this Congress laid the basis for this joint effort. We now must put into effect the common defense plans that are being worked out.

We shall continue our efforts for world economic recovery, because world prosperity is the only sure foundation of a permanent peace.

As an immediate means to this end we must continue our support of the European recovery program. This program has achieved great success in the first 2 years of its operation, but it has not yet been completed. If we were to stop this program now, or cripple it, just because it is succeeding, we should be doing exactly what the enemies of democracy want us to do. We should be just as foolish as a man who, for reasons of false economy, failed to put a roof on his house after building the foundation and the walls.

World prosperity also requires that we do all we can to expand world trade. As a major step in this direction we should promptly join the International Trade Organization. The purpose of this organization, which the United States has been foremost in creating, is to establish a code of fair practice, and an international authority for adjusting differences in international commercial relations. It is an effort to prevent the kind of anarchy and irresponsibility in world trade which did so much to bring about the world depression of the 1930's. An expanding world economy requires the improvement of living standards and the development of resources in areas where human poverty and misery now prevail. Without such improvement the recovery of Europe and the future of our own economy will not be secure. I urge that the Congress adopt the legislation now before it to provide for increasing the flow of technical assistance and capital investment in underdeveloped regions.

It is more essential now than ever, if the ideals of freedom and representative government are to prevail in these areas, and particularly in the Far East, that their peoples experience, in their own lives, the benefits of scientific and economic advances. This program will require the movement of large amounts of capital from the industrial nations, and particularly from the United States, to productive uses in the underdeveloped areas of the world. Recent world events make prompt action imperative.

This program is in the interest of all peoples-and has nothing in common with either the old imperialism of the last century or the new imperialism of the Communists.

Our aim for a peaceful, democratic world of free peoples will be achieved in the long run, not by force of arms, but by an appeal to the minds and hearts of men. If the peace policy of the democratic nations is to be successful, they must demonstrate that the benefits of their way of life can be increased and extended to all nations and all races.

In the world today we are confronted with the danger that the rising demand of people everywhere for freedom and a better life may be corrupted and betrayed by the false promises of communism. In its ruthless struggle for power, communism seizes upon our imperfections, and takes advantage of the delays and setbacks which the democratic nations experience in their effort to secure a better life for their citizens. This challenge to us is more than a military challenge. It is a challenge to the honesty of our profession of the democratic faith; it is a challenge to the efficiency and stability of our economic system; it is a challenge to the willingness to work with other peoples for world peace and for world prosperity.

For my part I welcome that challenge. I believe that our country, at this crucial point in world history, will meet that challenge successfully. I believe that, in cooperation with the other free nations of the world, we shall extend the full benefits of the democratic way of life to millions who do not now enjoy them, and preserve mankind from dictatorship and tyranny.

I believe that we shall succeed in our struggle for this peace, because I have seen the success we have had in our own country in following the principles of freedom. Over the last 50 years, the ideals of liberty and equal opportunity to which this Nation is dedicated have been increasingly realized in the lives of our people.

The ideal of equal opportunity no longer means simply the opportunity which a man has to advance beyond his fellows. Some of our citizens do achieve greater success than others as a reward for individual merit and effort, and this is as it should be. At the same time our country must be more than a land of opportunity for a select few. It must be a land of opportunity for all of us. In such a land we can grow and prosper together.

The simple truth that we can all go forward together is often questioned by selfish or shortsighted persons. It is strange that this is so, for this proposition is so clearly demonstrated by our national history. During the last 50 years, for example, our Nation has grown enormously in material well-being. This growth has come about, not by concentrating the benefits of our progress in the hands of a few, but by increasing the wealth of the great body of our Nation and our citizens.

In the last 50 years the income of the average family has increased so greatly that its buying power has doubled. The average hours of work have declined from 60 to 40 a week, the whole hourly production of the average worker has tripled. Average wages, allowing for price changes, have increased from about 45 cents an hour to $1.40 an hour.

We have accomplished what to earlier ages of mankind would have been a miracle—we work shorter hours, we produce more, and we live better.

Increasing freedom from poverty and drudgery has given a fuller meaning to American life. Our people are better educated; we have more opportunities for travel and recreation and enjoyment of the arts. We enjoy more personal liberty in the United States today than ever before.

If we can continue in the spirit of cooperative adventure which has marked the recent years of our progress, we can expect further scientific advances, further increases in our standard of living, and a still wider enjoyment of democratic freedom.

No one, of course, can foretell the future exactly. However, if we assume that we shall grow as fast in the future as we have grown in the past, we can get a good idea of how much our country should grow in the next 50 years.

At present our total national production is $255 billion a year. Our working population and our output per worker are increasing. If our productive power continues to increase at the same rate as it has increased over the past 50 years, our total national production 50 years from now will be nearly four times as much as it is today. Allowing for the expected growth in population, this would mean that the real income of the average family in the year 2000 A.D. would be about three times what it is today.

These are estimates of what we can do in the future, but we can reach these heights only if we follow the right policies. We have learned by bitter experience that progress is not automatic—that wrong policies lead to depression and disaster. We cannot achieve these gains unless we have a stable economy and avoid the catastrophes of boom and bust that have set us back in the past.

These gains cannot be achieved unless our businessmen maintain their spirit of initiative and enterprise and operate in a competitive economy. They cannot be achieved unless our workingmen and women and their unions help to increase productivity and obtain for labor a fair share of the benefits of our economic system. They cannot be achieved unless we have a stable and prosperous agriculture. They cannot be achieved unless we conserve and develop our natural resources in the public interest. Our system will not work unless our people are healthy, well-educated, and confident of the future. It will not work unless all citizens can participate fully in our national life.

In achieving these gains the Government has a special responsibility to help create and maintain the conditions which will permit the growth we know is possible. Foremost among these conditions is the need for a fair distribution of our increasing prosperity among all the great groups of our population who help to bring it about-labor, business, agriculture.

Businessmen must continue to have the incentives necessary for investment and for the development of new lines of enterprise. In the future growth of this country, lie possibilities for hundreds of thousands of new and independent businesses. As our national production increases, as it doubles and redoubles in the next 50 years, the number of independent and competing enterprises should also increase. If the number does not increase, our constantly growing economy will fall under the control of a few dominant economic groups whose powers will be so great that they will be a challenge to democratic institutions.

To avoid this danger, we must curb monopoly and provide aids to independent business so that it may have the credit and capital to compete in a system of free enterprise. I recommend that the Congress complete action at this session on the pending bill to close the loopholes in the Clayton Act which now permit monopolistic mergers. I also hope before this session is over to transmit to the Congress a series of proposals to strengthen the antimonopoly laws, to assist small business, and to encourage the growth of new enterprises.

In the case of labor, free collective bargaining must be protected and encouraged. Collective bargaining is not only a fundamental economic freedom for labor. It is also a strengthening and stabilizing influence for our whole economy.

The Federal statute now governing labor relations is punitive in purpose and one-sided in operation. This statute is, and always has been, inconsistent with the practice of true and effective collective bargaining. It should be repealed and replaced by a law that is fair to all and in harmony with our democratic ideals.

A full understanding of the problems of modern labor relations is of such importance that I recommend the establishment of a labor extension service to encourage educational activities in this field.

Another essential for our continued growth is a stable and prosperous agriculture. For many years we have been building a program to give the farmer a reasonable measure of protection against the special hazards to which he is exposed. That program was improved at the last session of the Congress. However, our farm legislation is still not adequate.

Although the Congress has properly declared as a matter of national policy that safeguards must be maintained against slumps in farm prices, there are serious shortcomings in the methods now available for carrying out this policy. Mandatory price supports should be provided for the commodities not now covered which are major sources of farm income.

Moreover, we should provide a method of supporting farm income at fair levels which will, at the same time, avoid piling up unmanageable surpluses and allow consumers to obtain the full benefit of our abundant agricultural production. A system of production payments gives the greatest promise of accomplishing this purpose. I recommend that the use of such a system be authorized.

One of the most important factors in our continued growth is the construction of more good, up-to-date housing. In a country such as ours there is no reason why decent homes should not be within the reach of all. With the help of various Government programs we have made great progress in the last few years in increasing the number of homes.

Despite this increase, there is still an acute shortage of housing for the lower and middle-income groups, especially in large metropolitan areas. We have laid the groundwork for relieving the plight of lower-income families in the Housing Act of 1949. To aid the middle-income families, I recommend that the Congress enact new legislation authorizing a vigorous program to help cooperatives and other nonprofit groups build housing which these families can afford.

Rent control has done a great deal to prevent the housing shortage from having had worse effects during this postwar period of adjustment. Rent control is still necessary to prevent widespread hardship and sharp curtailment of the buying power of millions of consumers in metropolitan areas. I recommend, therefore, that rent control be continued for another year.

If we are to achieve a better life for all, the natural resources of the country must be regarded as a public trust. We must use our precious assets of soil, water, and forest, and grassland in such a way that they become constantly more productive and more valuable. Government investment in the conservation and development of our resources is necessary to the future economic expansion of the country.

We need to enlarge the production and transmission of public power. That is true not only in those regions which have already received great benefits from Federal power projects, but also in regions such as New England where the benefits of large-scale public power development have not yet been experienced.

In our hydroelectric and irrigation undertakings, as well as in our other resource programs, we must continue policies to assure that their benefits will be spread among the many and not restricted to the favored few.

Important resource legislation which should be passed at this session includes the authorization of the St. Lawrence seaway and power project and the establishment of the Columbia Valley Administration—the establishment of the Columbia Valley Administration, I don't want you to miss that.

Through wise Government policies and Government expenditures for the conservation and development of our natural resources, we can be sure of transmitting to our children and our children's children a country far richer and more productive than the one we know today.

The value of our natural resources is constantly being increased by the progress of science. Research is finding new ways of using such natural assets as minerals, sea water, and plant life. In the peaceful development of atomic energy, particularly, we stand on the threshold of new wonders. The first experimental machines for producing useful power from atomic energy are now under construction. We have made only the first beginnings in this field, but in the perspective of history they may loom larger than the first airplane, or even the first tools that started man on the road to civilization.

To take full advantage of the increasing possibilities of nature we must equip ourselves with increasing knowledge. Government has a responsibility to see that our country maintains its position in the advance of science. As a step toward this end, the Congress should complete action on the measure to create a National Science Foundation.

Another duty of the Government is to promote the economic security, the health, and the education of its citizens. By so doing, we strengthen both our economy and the structure of our society. In a nation as rich as ours, all citizens should be able to live in decency and health.

Our Social Security System should be developed into the main reliance of our people for basic protection against the economic hazards of old-age, unemployment, and illness. I earnestly hope that the Congress will complete action at this session on legislation to increase the benefits and extend the coverage of old-age and survivors' insurance. The widespread movement to provide pensions in private industry dramatizes the need for improvements in the public insurance system.

I also urge that the Congress strengthen our unemployment compensation law to meet present-day needs more adequately. The economic downturn of the past year was the first real test that our system of unemployment insurance has had to meet. That test has proved the wisdom of the system, but it has also made strikingly apparent the need for improving its operation and increasing its coverage and its benefits.

In the field of health there are immense opportunities to extend to more of our people the benefits of the amazing advances in medical science. We have made a good beginning in expanding our hospitals, but we must also go on to remedy the shortages of doctors, nurses, and public health services, and to establish a system of medical insurance which will enable all Americans to afford good medical care.

We must take immediate steps to strengthen our educational system. In many parts of our country, young people are being handicapped for life because of a poor education. The rapidly increasing number of children of school age, coupled with the shortage of qualified teachers, makes this problem more critical each year. I believe that the Congress should no longer delay in providing Federal assistance to the States so that they can maintain adequate schools.

As we go forward in achieving greater economic security and greater opportunity for all our people, we should make every effort to extend the benefits of our democratic institutions to every citizen. The religious ideals which we profess, and the heritage of freedom which we have received from the past, clearly place that duty upon us. I again urge the Congress to enact the civil rights proposals I made in February 1948. These proposals are for the enactment of Federal statutes which will protect all our people in the exercise of their democratic rights and their search for economic opportunity, grant statehood to Alaska and Hawaii, provide a greater measure of self-government for our island possessions, and accord home rule to the District of Columbia. Some of those proposals have been before the Congress for a long time. Those who oppose them, as well as those who favor them, should recognize that it is the duty of the elected representatives of the people to let these proposals come to a vote.

Our democratic ideals, as well as our best interests, require that we do our fair share in providing homes for the unfortunate victims of war and tyranny. In so doing, we shall add strength to our democracy through the abilities and skills which these men and women will bring here. I urge the prompt enactment by the Congress of the legislation now before it to extend and broaden the existing displaced persons law and remove its discriminatory features.

The measures I am recommending to the Congress concerning both our foreign and our domestic policies represent a carefully considered program to meet our national needs. It is a program which necessarily requires large expenditures of funds. More than 70 percent of the Government's expenditures are required to meet the costs of past wars and to work for world peace. This is the dominant factor in our fiscal policy. At the same time, the Government must make substantial expenditures which are necessary to the growth and expansion of the domestic economy.

At present, largely because of the ill-considered tax reduction of the Both Congress, the Government is not receiving enough revenue to meet its necessary expenditures.

To meet this situation, I am proposing that Federal expenditures be held to the lowest levels consistent with our international requirements and the essential needs of economic growth, and the well-being of our people. I think I had better read that over; you interrupted me in the middle.

To meet this situation, I am proposing that Federal expenditures be held to the lowest levels consistent with our international requirements and the essential needs of economic growth, and the well-being of our people. Don't forget that last phrase. At the same time, we must guard against the folly of attempting budget slashes which would impair our prospects for peace or cripple the programs essential to our national strength.

The budget recommendations I shall shortly transmit to the Congress show that we can expect a substantial improvement in our fiscal position over the next few years, as the cost of some of our extraordinary postwar programs declines, and as the Government revenue rises as a result of growth in employment and national income. To further improve our fiscal outlook, we should make some changes in our tax system which will reduce present inequities, stimulate business activity, and yield a moderate amount of additional revenue. I expect to transmit specific recommendations to the Congress on this subject at a very early date.

The fiscal policy I am recommending is the quickest and safest way of achieving a balanced budget.

As we move forward into the second half of the 20th century, we must always bear in mind the central purpose of our national life. We do not seek material prosperity for ourselves because we love luxury; we do not aid other nations because we wish to increase our power. We have not devised programs for the security and well-being of our people because we are afraid or unwilling to take risks. This is not the meaning of our past history or our present course.

We work for a better life for all, so that all men may put to good use the great gifts with which they have been endowed by their Creator. We seek to establish those material conditions of life in which, without exception, men may live in dignity, perform useful work, serve their communities, and worship God as they see fit.

These may seem simple goals, but they are not little ones. They are worth a great deal more than all the empires and conquests of history. They are not to be achieved by military aggression or political fanaticism. They are to be achieved by humbler means-by hard work, by a spirit of self-restraint in our dealings with one another, and by a deep devotion to the principles of justice and equality.

It should make us truly thankful, as we look back to the beginnings of this country, that we have come so far along the road to a better life for all. It should make us humble to think, as we look ahead, how much farther we have to go to accomplish, at home and abroad, the objectives that were set out for us at the founding of this great Nation.

As we approach the halfway mark of the 20th century, we should ask for continued strength and guidance from that Almighty Power who has placed before us such great opportunities for the good of mankind in the years to come.

State of the Union Address Harry S. Truman

January 8, 1951

Mr. President, Mr. Speaker, Members of the Congress:

This 82d Congress faces as grave a task as any Congress in the history of our Republic. The actions you take will be watched by the whole world. These actions will measure the ability of a free people, acting through their chosen representatives and their free institutions, to meet a deadly challenge to their way of life.

We can meet this challenge foolishly or wisely. We can meet it timidly or bravely, shamefully or honorably.

I know that the 82d Congress will meet this challenge in a way worthy of our great heritage. I know that your debates will be earnest, responsible, constructive, and to the point. I know that from these debates there will come the great decisions needed to carry us forward.

At this critical time, I am glad to say that our country is in a healthy condition. Our democratic institutions are sound and strong. We have more men and women at work than ever before. We are able to produce more than ever before—in fact, far more than any country ever produced in the history of the world.

I am confident that we can succeed in the great task that lies before us.

We will succeed, but we must all do our part. We must all act together as citizens of this great Republic.

As we meet here today, American soldiers are fighting a bitter campaign in Korea. We pay tribute to their courage, devotion, and gallantry.

Our men are fighting, alongside their United Nations allies, because they know, as we do, that the aggression in Korea is part of the attempt of the Russian Communist dictatorship to take over the world, step by step.

Our men are fighting a long way from home, but they are fighting for our lives and our liberties. They are fighting to protect our right to meet here today—our right to govern ourselves as a free nation.

The threat of world conquest by Soviet Russia endangers our liberty and endangers the kind of world in which the free spirit of man can survive. This threat is aimed at all peoples who strive to win or defend their own freedom and national independence.

Indeed, the state of our Nation is in great part the state of our friends and allies throughout the world. The gun that points at them points at us, also. The threat is a total threat and the danger is a common danger.

All free nations are exposed and all are in peril. Their only security lies in banding together. No one nation can find protection in a selfish search for a safe haven from the storm.

The free nations do not have any aggressive purpose. We want only peace in the world—peace for all countries. No threat to the security of any nation is concealed in our plans and programs.

We had hoped that the Soviet Union, with its security assured by the Charter of the United Nations, would be willing to live and let live. But I am sorry to say that has not been the case.

The imperialism of the czars has been replaced by the even more ambitious, more crafty, and more menacing imperialism of the rulers of the Soviet Union.

This new imperialism has powerful military forces. It is keeping millions of men under arms. It has a large air force and a strong submarine force. It has complete control of the men and equipment of its satellites. It has kept its subject peoples and its economy in a state of perpetual mobilization.

The present rulers of the Soviet Union have shown that they are willing to use this power to destroy the free nations and win domination over the whole world.

The Soviet imperialists have two ways of going about their destructive work. They use the method of subversion and internal revolution, and they use the method of external aggression. In preparation for either of these methods of attack, they stir up class strife and disorder. They encourage sabotage. They put out poisonous propaganda. They deliberately try to prevent economic improvement.

If their efforts are successful, they foment a revolution, as they did in Czechoslovakia and China, and as they tried, unsuccessfully, to do in Greece. If their methods of subversion are blocked, and if they think they can get away with outright warfare, they resort to external aggression. This is what they did when they loosed the armies of their puppet states against the Republic of Korea, in an evil war by proxy.

We of the free world must be ready to meet both of these methods of Soviet action. We must not neglect one or the other.

The free world has power and resources to meet these two forms of aggression—resources that are far greater than those of the Soviet dictatorship. We have skilled and vigorous peoples, great industrial strength, and abundant sources of raw materials. And above all, we cherish liberty. Our common ideals are a great part of our strength. These ideals are the driving force of human progress.

The free nations believe in the dignity and the worth of man.

We believe in independence for all nations.

We believe that free and independent nations can band together into a world order based on law. We have laid the cornerstone of such a peaceful world in the United Nations.

We believe that such a world order can and should spread the benefits of modern science and industry, better health and education, more food and rising standards of living—throughout the world.

These ideals give our cause a power and vitality that Russian communism can never command.

The free nations, however, are bound together by more than ideals. They are a real community bound together also by the ties of self-interest and self-preservation. If they should fall apart, the results would be fatal to human freedom.

Our own national security is deeply involved with that of the other free nations. While they need our support, we equally need theirs. Our national safety would be gravely prejudiced if the Soviet Union were to succeed in harnessing to its war machine the resources and the manpower of the free nations on the borders of its empire.

If Western Europe were to fall to Soviet Russia, it would double the Soviet supply of coal and triple the Soviet supply of steel. If the free countries of Asia and Africa should fall to Soviet Russia, we would lose the sources of many of our most vital raw materials, including uranium, which is the basis of our atomic power. And Soviet command of the manpower of the free nations of Europe and Asia would confront us with military forces which we could never hope to equal.

In such a situation, the Soviet Union could impose its demands on the world, without resort to conflict, simply through the preponderance of its economic and military power. The Soviet Union does not have to attack the United States to secure domination of the world. It can achieve its ends by isolating us and swallowing up all our allies. Therefore, even if we were craven enough I do not believe we could be—but, I say, even if we were craven enough to abandon our ideals, it would be disastrous for us to withdraw from the community of free nations.

We are the most powerful single member of this community, and we have a special responsibility. We must take the leadership in meeting the challenge to freedom and in helping to protect the rights of independent nations.

This country has a practical, realistic program of action for meeting this challenge.

First, we shall have to extend economic assistance, where it can be effective. The best way to stop subversion by the Kremlin is to strike at the roots of social injustice and economic disorder. People who have jobs, homes, and hopes for the future will defend themselves against the underground agents of the Kremlin. Our programs of economic aid have done much to turn back Communism,

In Europe the Marshall plan has had an electrifying result. As European recovery progressed, the strikes led by the Kremlin's agents in Italy and France failed. All over Western Europe the Communist Party took worse and worse beatings at the polls.

The countries which have received Marshall plan aid have been able, through hard work, to expand their productive strength-in many cases, to levels higher than ever before in their history. Without this strength they would be completely incapable of defending themselves today. They are now ready to use this strength in helping to build a strong combined defense against aggression.

We shall need to continue some economic aid to European countries. This aid should now be specifically related to the building of their defenses.

In other parts of the world our economic assistance will need to be more broadly directed toward economic development. In the Near East, in Africa, in Asia, we must do what we can to help people who are striving to advance from misery, poverty, and hunger. We must also continue to help the economic growth of our good neighbors in this hemisphere. These actions will bring greater strength for the free world. They will give many people a real stake in the future and reason to defend their freedom. They will mean increased production of goods they need and materials we need.

Second, we shall need to continue our military assistance to countries which want to defend themselves.

The heart of our common defense effort is the North Atlantic community. The defense of Europe is the basis for the defense of the whole free world—ourselves included. Next to the United States, Europe is the largest workshop in the world. It is also a homeland of the great religious beliefs shared by many of our citizens beliefs which are now threatened by the tide of atheistic communism.

Strategically, economically, and morally, the defense of Europe is a part of our own defense. That is why we have joined with the countries of Europe in the North Atlantic Treaty, pledging ourselves to work with them.

There has been much discussion recently over whether the European countries are willing to defend themselves. Their actions are answering this question.

Our North Atlantic Treaty partners have strict systems of universal military training. Several have recently increased the term of service. All have taken measures to improve the quality of training. Forces are being trained and expanded as rapidly as the necessary arms and equipment can be supplied from their factories and ours. Our North Atlantic Treaty partners, together, are building armies bigger than our own.

None of the North Atlantic Treaty countries, including our

own country, has done enough yet. But real progress is being made. Together, we have worked out defense 'plans. The military leaders of our own country took part in working out these plans, and are agreed that they are sound and within our capabilities.

To put these plans into action, we sent to Europe last week one of our greatest military commanders, General Dwight D. Eisenhower.

General Eisenhower went to Europe to assume command of the united forces of the North Atlantic Treaty countries, including our own forces in Germany.

The people of Europe have confidence in General Eisenhower. They know his ability to put together a fighting force of allies. His mission is vital to our security. We should all stand behind him, and give him every bit of help we can.

Part of our job will be to reinforce the military strength of our European partners by sending them weapons and equipment as our military production expands.

Our program of military assistance extends to the nations in the Near East and the Far East which are trying to defend their freedom. Soviet communism is trying to make these nations into colonies, and to use their people as cannon fodder in new wars of conquest. We want their people to be free men and to enjoy peace.

Our country has always stood for freedom for the peoples of Asia. Long, long ago it stood for the freedom of the peoples of Asia. Our history shows this. We have demonstrated it in the Philippines. We have demonstrated it in our relations with Indonesia, India, and with China. We hope to join in restoring the people of Japan to membership in the community of free nations.

It is in the Far East that we have taken up arms, under the United Nations, to preserve the principle of independence for free nations. We are fighting to keep the forces of Communist aggression from making a slave state out of Korea.

Korea has tremendous significance for the world. It means that free nations, acting through the United Nations, are fighting together against aggression.

We will understand the importance of this best if we look back into history. If the democracies had stood up against the invasion of Manchuria in 1931, or the attack on Ethiopia in 1935, or the seizure of Austria in 1938, if they had stood together against aggression on those occasions as the United Nations has done in Korea, the whole history of our time would have been different.

The principles for which we are fighting in Korea are right and just. They are the foundations of collective security and of the future of free nations. Korea is not only a country undergoing the torment of aggression; it is also a symbol. It stands for right and justice in the world against oppression and slavery. The free world must always stand for these principles—and we will stand with the free world.

As the third part of our program, we will continue to work for peaceful settlements in international disputes. We will support the United Nations and remain loyal to the great principles of international cooperation laid down in its charter.

We are willing, as we have always been, to negotiate honorable settlements with the Soviet Union. But we will not engage in appeasement.

The Soviet rulers have made it clear that we must have strength as well as right on our side. If we build our strength—and we are building it—the Soviet rulers may face the facts and lay aside their plans to take over the world.

That is what we hope will happen, and that is what we are trying to bring about. That is the only realistic road to peace.

These are the main elements of the course our Nation must follow as a member of the community of free nations. These are the things we must do to preserve our security and help create a peaceful world. But they will be successful only if we increase the strength of our own country.

Here at home we have some very big jobs to do. We are building much stronger military forces—and we are building them fast. We are preparing for full wartime mobilization, if that should be necessary. And we are continuing to build a strong and growing economy, able to maintain whatever effort may be required for as long as necessary.

We are building our own Army, Navy, and Air Force to an active strength of nearly 3 1/2 million men and women. We are stepping up the training of the reserve forces, and establishing more training facilities, so that we can rapidly increase our active forces far more on short notice.

We are going to produce all the weapons and equipment that such an armed force will need. Furthermore, we will make weapons for our allies, and weapons for our own reserve supplies. On top of this, we will build the capacity to turn out on short notice arms and supplies that may be needed for a full-scale war.

Fortunately, we have a good start on this because of our enormous plant capacity and because of the equipment on hand from the last war. For example, many combat ships are being returned to active duty from the "mothball fleet" and many others can be put into service on very short notice. We have large reserves of arms and ammunition and thousands of workers skilled in arms production.

In many cases, however, our stocks of weapons are low. In other cases, those on hand are not the most modern. We have made remarkable technical advances. We have developed new types of jet planes and powerful new tanks. We are concentrating on producing the newest types of weapons and producing them as fast as we can.

This production drive is more selective than the one we had during World War II, but it is just as urgent and intense. It is a big program and it is a costly one.

Let me give you two concrete examples. Our present program calls for expanding the aircraft industry so that it will have the capacity to produce 50,000 modern military planes a year. We are preparing the capacity to produce 35,000 tanks a year. We are not now ordering that many planes or that many tanks, and we hope that we never have to, but we mean to be able to turn them out if we need them.

The planes we are producing now are much bigger, much better, and much more expensive than the planes we had during the last war.

We used to think that the B-17 was a huge plane, and the blockbuster it carried a huge load. But the B-36 can carry five of these blockbusters in its belly, and it can carry them five times as far. Of course, the B-36 is much more complicated to build than the B-17, and far more expensive. One B-17 costs $275,000, while now one B-36 costs $3 ½ million.

I ask you to remember that what we are doing is to provide the best and most modern military equipment in the world for our fighting forces.

This kind of defense production program has two parts.

The first part is to get our defense production going as fast as possible. We have to convert plants and channel materials to defense production. This means heavy cuts in civilian uses of copper, aluminum, rubber, and other essential materials. It means shortages in various consumer goods.

The second part is to increase our capacity to produce and to keep our economy strong for the long pull. We do not know how long Communist aggression will threaten the world.

Only by increasing our output can we carry the burden of preparedness for an indefinite period in the future. This means that we will have to build more power plants and more steel mills, grow more cotton, mine more copper, and expand our capacity in many other ways.

The Congress will need to consider legislation, at this session, affecting all the aspects of our mobilization job. The main subjects on which legislation will be needed are:

First, appropriations for our military buildup.

Second, extension and revision of the Selective Service Act.

Third, military and economic aid to help build up the strength of the free world.

Fourth, revision and extension of the authority to expand production and to stabilize prices, wages, and rents.

Fifth, improvement of our agricultural laws to help obtain the kinds of farm products we need for the defense effort.

Sixth, improvement of our labor laws to help provide stable labor-management relations and to make sure that we have steady production in this emergency.

Seventh, housing and training of defense workers and the full use of all our manpower resources.

Eighth, means for increasing the supply of doctors, nurses, and other trained medical personnel critically needed for the defense effort.

Ninth, aid to the States to meet the most urgent needs of our elementary and secondary schools. Some of our plans will have to be deferred for the time being. But we should do all we can to make sure our children are being trained as good and useful citizens in the critical times ahead.

Tenth, a major increase in taxes to meet the cost of the defense effort.

The Economic Report and the Budget Message will discuss these subjects further. In addition, I shall send to the Congress special messages containing detailed recommendations on legislation needed at this Session.

In the months ahead the Government must give priority to activities that are urgent—like military procurement and atomic energy and power development. It must practice rigid economy in its nondefense activities. Many of the things we would normally do must be curtailed or postponed.

But in a long-term defense effort like this one, we cannot neglect the measures needed to maintain a strong economy and a healthy democratic society.

The Congress, therefore, should give continued attention to the measures which our country will need for the long pull. And it should act upon such legislation as promptly as circumstances permit.

To take just one example—we need to continue and complete the work of rounding out our system of social insurance. We still need to improve our protection against unemployment and old age. We still need to provide insurance against the loss of earnings through sickness, and against the high costs of modern medical care.

And above all, we must remember that the fundamentals of our strength rest upon the freedoms of our people. We must continue our efforts to achieve the full realization of our democratic ideals. We must uphold the freedom of speech and the freedom of conscience in our land. We must assure equal rights and equal opportunities to all our citizens.

As we go forward this year in the defense of freedom, let us keep dearly before us the nature of our present effort.

We are building up our strength, in concert with other free nations, to meet the danger of aggression that has been turned loose on the world. The strength of the free nations is the world's best hope of peace.

I ask the Congress for unity in these crucial days.

Make no mistake about my meaning. I do not ask, or expect, unanimity. I do not ask for an end to debate. Only by debate can we arrive at decisions which are wise, and which reflect the desires of the American people. We do not have a dictatorship in this country, and we never will have one in this country.

When I request unity, what I am really asking for is a sense of responsibility on the part of every Member of this Congress. Let us debate the issues, but let every man among us weigh his words and his deeds. There is a sharp difference between harmful criticism and constructive criticism. If we are truly responsible as individuals, I am sure that we will be unified as a government.

Let us keep our eyes on the issues and work for the things we all believe in.

Let each of us put our country ahead of our party, and ahead of our own personal interests.

I had the honor to be a Member of the Senate during World War II, and I know from experience that unity of purpose and of effort is possible in the Congress without any lessening of the vitality of our two-party system.

Let us all stand together as Americans. Let us stand together with all men everywhere who believe in human liberty.

Peace is precious to us. It is the way of life we strive for with all the strength and wisdom we possess. But more precious than peace are freedom and justice. We will fight, if fight we must, to keep our freedom and to prevent justice from being destroyed.

These are the things that give meaning to our lives, and

which we acknowledge to be greater than ourselves.

This is our cause—peace, freedom, justice. We will pursue this cause with determination and humility, asking divine guidance that in all we do we may follow the will of God.

State of the Union Address Harry S. Truman

January 9, 1952

Mr. President, Mr. Speaker, Members of the Congress:

I have the honor to report to the Congress on the state of the Union.

At the outset, I should like to speak of the necessity for putting first things first as we work together this year for the good of our country.

The United States and the whole free world are passing through a period of grave danger. Every action you take here in Congress, and every action that I take as President, must be measured against the test of whether it helps to meet that danger.

This will be a presidential election year-the year in which politics plays a large part in our lives—a larger part than usual. That is perfectly proper. But we have a greater responsibility to conduct our political fights in a manner that does not harm the national interest.

We can find plenty of things to differ about without destroying our free institutions and without abandoning our bipartisan foreign policy for peace.

When everything is said and done, all of us—Republicans and Democrats alike—all of us are Americans; and we are all going to sink or swim together.

We are moving through a perilous time. Faced with a terrible threat of aggression, our Nation has embarked upon a great effort to help establish the kind of world in which peace shall be secure. Peace is our goal-not peace at any price, but a peace based on freedom and justice. We are now in the midst of our effort to reach that goal. On the whole, we have been doing very well.

Last year, 1951, was a year in which we threw back aggression, added greatly to our military strength, and improved the chances for peace and freedom in many parts of the world.

This year, 1952, is a critical year in the defense effort of the whole free world. If we falter we can lose all the gains we have made. If we drive ahead, with courage and vigor and determination, we can by the end of 1952 be in a position of much greater security. The way will be dangerous for the years ahead, but if we put forth our best efforts this year—and next year—we can be "over the hump" in our effort to build strong defenses.

When we look at the record of the past year, 1951, we find important things on both the credit and the debit side of the ledger. We have made great advances. At the same time we have run into new problems which must be overcome.

Now let us look at the credit side first.

Peace depends upon the free nations sticking together, and making a combined effort to check aggression and prevent war. In this respect, 1951 was a year of great achievement.

In Korea the forces of the United Nations turned hack the Chinese Communist invasion-and did it without widening the area of conflict. The action of the United Nations in Korea has been a powerful deterrent to a third world war. However, the situation in Korea remains very hazardous. The outcome of the armistice negotiation still remains uncertain.

In Indochina and Malaya, our aid has helped our allies to hold back the Communist advance, although there are signs of further trouble in that area.

In 1951 we strengthened the chances of peace in the Pacific region by the treaties with Japan and the defense arrangements with Australia, New Zealand, and the Philippines.

In Europe combined defense has become a reality. The free nations have created a real fighting force. This force is not yet as strong as it needs to be; but it is already a real obstacle to any attempt by hostile forces to sweep across Europe to the Atlantic.

In 1951 we also moved to strengthen the security of Europe by the agreement to bring Greece and Turkey into the North Atlantic Treaty.

The United Nations, the world's greatest hope for peace, has come through a year of trial stronger and more useful than ever. The free nations have stood together in blocking Communist attempts to tear up the charter.

At the present session of the United Nations in Paris, we, together with the British and the French, offered a plan to reduce and control all armaments under a foolproof inspection system. This is a concrete, practical proposal for disarmament.

But what happened ? Vishinsky laughed at it. Listen to what he said: "I could hardly sleep at all last night .... I could not sleep because I kept laughing." The world will be a long time forgetting the spectacle of that fellow laughing at disarmament.

Disarmament is not a joke. Vishinsky's laughter met with shock and anger from the people all over the world. And, as a result, Mr. Stalin's representative received orders to stop laughing and start talking.

If the Soviet leaders were to accept this proposal, it would lighten the burden of armaments, and permit the resources of the earth to be devoted to the good of mankind. But until the Soviet Union accepts a sound disarmament proposal, and joins in peaceful settlements, we have no choice except to build up our defenses.

During this past year we added more than a million men and women to our Armed Forces. The total is now nearly 3 ½ million. We have made rapid progress in the field of atomic weapons. We have turned out billion worth of military supplies and equipment, three times as much as the year before.

Economic conditions in the country are good. There are 61 million people on the job; wages, farm incomes, and business profits are at high levels. Total production of goods and services in our country has increased 8 percent over last year—about twice the normal rate of growth.

Perhaps the most amazing thing about our economic progress is the way we are increasing our basic capacity to produce. For example, we are now in the second year of a 3-year program which will double our output of aluminum, increase our electric power supply by 40 percent, and increase our steelmaking capacity by 15 percent. We can then produce 120 million tons of steel a year, as much as all the rest of the world put together.

This expansion will mean more jobs and higher standards of living for all of us in the years ahead. At the present time it means greater strength for us and for the rest of the free world in the fight for peace.

Now, I must turn to the debit side of the ledger for the past year.

The outstanding fact to note on the debit side of the ledger is that the Soviet Union, in 1951, continued to expand its military production and increase its already excessive military power.

It is true that the Soviets have run into increasing difficulties. Their hostile policies have awakened stern resistance among free men throughout the world. And behind the Iron Curtain the Soviet rule of force has created growing political and economic stresses in the satellite nations.

Nevertheless, the grim fact remains that the Soviet Union is increasing its armed might. It is still producing more war planes than the free nations. It has set off two more atomic explosions. The world still walks in the shadow of another world war.

And here at home, our defense preparations are far from complete.

During 1951 we did not make adequate progress in building up civil defense against atomic attack. This is a major weakness in our plans for peace, since inadequate civilian defense is an open invitation to a surprise attack. Failure to provide adequate civilian defense has the same effect as adding to the enemy's supply of atomic bombs.

In the field of defense production we have run into difficulties and delays in designing and producing the latest types of airplanes and tanks. Some machine tools and metals are still in extremely short supply.

In other free countries the defense buildup has created severe economic problems. It has increased inflation in Europe and has endangered the continued recovery of our allies.

In the Middle East political tensions and the oil controversy in Iran are keeping the region in a turmoil. In the Far East the dark threat of Communist imperialism still hangs over many nations.

This, very briefly, is the good side and the bad side of the picture.

Taking the good and bad together, we have made real progress this last year along the road to peace. We have increased the power and unity of the free world. And while we were doing this, we have avoided world war on the one hand, and appeasement on the other. This is a hard road to follow, but the events of the last year show that it is the right road to peace.

We cannot expect to complete the job overnight. The free nations may have to maintain for years the larger military forces needed to deter aggression. We must build steadily, over a period of years, toward political solidarity and economic progress among the free nations in all parts of the world.

Our task will not be easy; but if we go at it with a will, we can look forward to steady progress. On our side are all the great resources of freedom—the ideals of religion and democracy, the aspiration of people for a better life, and the industrial and technical power of a free civilization.

These advantages outweigh anything the slave world can produce. The only thing that can defeat us is our own state of mind. We can lose if we falter.

The middle period of a great national effort like this is a very difficult time. The way seems long and hard. The goal seems far distant. Some people get discouraged. That is only natural.

But if there are any among us who think we ought to ease up in the fight for peace, I want to remind them of three things—just three things.

First: The threat of world war is still very real. We had one Pearl Harbor—let's not get caught off guard again. If you don't think the threat of Communist armies is real, talk to some of our men back from Korea.

Second: If the United States had to try to stand alone against a Soviet-dominated world, it would destroy the life we know and the ideals we hold dear. Our allies are essential to us, just as we are essential to them. The more shoulders there are to bear the burden the lighter that burden will be.

Third: The things we believe in most deeply are under relentless attack. We have the great responsibility of saving the basic moral and spiritual values of our civilization. We have started out well—with a program for peace that is unparalleled in history. If we believe in ourselves and the faith we profess, we will stick to that job until it is victoriously finished.

This is a time for courage, not for grumbling and mumbling.

Now, let us take a look at the things we have to do.

The thing that is uppermost in the minds of all of us is the situation in Korea. We must, and we will, keep up the fight there until we get the kind of armistice that will put an end to the aggression and protect the safety of our forces and the security of the Republic of Korea. Beyond that we shall continue to work for a settlement in Korea that upholds the principles of the United Nations.

We went into Korea because we knew that Communist aggression had to be met firmly if freedom was to be preserved in the world. We went into the fight to save the Republic of Korea, a free country, established under the United Nations. These are our aims. We will not give up until we attain them.

Meanwhile, we must continue to strengthen the forces of freedom throughout the world.

I hope the Senate will take early and favorable action on the

Japanese peace treaty, on our security pacts with the Pacific countries, and on the agreement to bring Greece and Turkey into the North Atlantic Treaty.

We are also negotiating an agreement with the German Federal Republic under which it can play an honorable and equal part among nations and take its place in the defense of Western Europe.

But treaties and plans are only the skeleton of our defense structure. The sinew and muscle of defense are the forces and equipment which must be provided.

In Europe we must go on helping our friends and allies to build up their military forces. This means we must send weapons in large volume to our European allies. I have directed that weapons for Europe be given a very high priority. Economic aid is necessary, too, to supply the margin of difference between success and failure in making Europe a strong partner in our joint defense.

In the long run we want to see Europe freed from any dependence on our aid. Our European allies want that just as bad as we do. The steps that are now being taken to build European unity should help bring that about. Six European countries are pooling their coal and steel production under the Schuman plan. Work is going forward on the merger of European national forces on the Continent into a single army. These great projects should become realities in 1952.

We should do all we can to help and encourage the move toward a strong and united Europe.

In Asia the new Communist empire is a daily threat to millions of people. The peoples of Asia want to be free to follow their own way of life. They want to preserve their culture and their traditions against communism, just as much as we want to preserve ours. They are laboring under terrific handicaps—poverty, ill health, feudal systems of land ownership, and the threat of internal subversion or external attack. We can and we must increase our help to them.

This means military aid, especially to those places like Indochina which might be hardest hit by some new Communist attack.

It also means economic aid, both technical know-how and capital investment.

This last year we made available millions of bushels of wheat to relieve famine in India. But far more important, in the long run, is the work Americans are doing in India to help the Indian farmers themselves raise more grain. With the help of our technicians, Indian farmers, using simple, inexpensive means, have been able since 1948 to double the crops in one area in India. One farmer there raised 63 bushels of wheat to the acre, where 13 bushels had been the average before.

This is point 4—our point 4 program at work. It is working—not only in India but in Iran, Paraguay, Liberia—in 33 countries around the globe. Our technical missionaries are out there. We need more of them. We need more funds to speed their efforts, because there is nothing of greater importance in all our foreign policy. There is nothing that shows more clearly what we stand for, and what we want to achieve.

My friends of the Congress, less than one-third of the expenditure for the cost of World War II would have created the developments necessary to feed the whole world so we wouldn't have to stomach communism. That is what we have got to fight, and unless we fight that battle and win it, we can't win the cold war or a hot one either.

We have recently lost a great public servant who was leading this effort to bring opportunity and hope to the people of half the world. Dr. Henry Bennett and his associates died in line of duty on a point 4 mission. It is up to us to carry on the great work for which they gave their lives.

During the coming year we must not forget the suffering of the people who live behind the Iron Curtain. In those areas minorities are being oppressed, human rights violated, religions persecuted. We should continue to expose those wrongs. We should continue and expand the activities of the Voice of America, which brings our message of hope and truth to those peoples and other peoples throughout the world.

I have just had an opportunity to discuss many of these world problems with Prime Minister Churchill. We have had a most satisfactory series of meetings. We thoroughly reviewed the situation in Europe, the Middle East, and the Far East. We both look forward to steady progress toward peace through the cooperative action and teamwork of the free nations.

Turning from our foreign policies, let us consider the jobs we have here at home as a part of our program for peace.

The first of these jobs is to move ahead full steam on the defense program.

Our objective is to have a well-equipped active defense force large enough—in concert with the forces of our allies—to deter aggression and to inflict punishing losses on the enemy immediately if we should be attacked. This active force must be backed by adequate reserves, and by the plants and tools to turn out the tremendous quantities of new weapons that would be needed if war came. We are not building an active force adequate to carry on full scale war, but we are putting ourselves in a position to mobilize very rapidly if we have to.

This year I shall recommend some increases in the size of the active force we are building, with particular emphasis on air power. This means we shall have to continue large-scale production of planes and other equipment for a longer period of time than we had originally planned.

Planes and tanks and other weapons-what the military call "hard goods"—are now beginning to come off the production lines in volume. Deliveries of hard goods now amount to about a billion and a half dollars worth a month. A year from now, we expect that rate to be doubled.

We shall have to hold to a high rate of military output for about a year after that. In 1954 we hope to have enough equipment so that we can reduce the production of most military items substantially. The next 2 years should therefore be the peak period of defense production.

Defense needs will take a lot of steel, aluminum, copper, nickel, and other scarce materials. This means smaller production of some civilian goods. The cutbacks will be nothing like those during World War II, when most civilian production was completely stopped. But there will be considerably less of some goods than we have been used to these past 2 or 3 years.

The very critical part of our defense job this year is to keep down inflation.

We can control inflation if we make up our minds to do it.

On the executive side of the Government, we intend to hold the line on prices just as tightly as the law allows. We will permit only those wage increases which are clearly justified under sound stabilization policies; and we will see to it that industries absorb cost increases out of earnings wherever feasible, before they are authorized to raise prices. We will do that, at any rate, except where the recent amendments to the law specifically require us to give further price increases.

Congress has a tremendous responsibility in this matter. Our stabilization law was shot full of holes at the last session. This year, it will be one of the main tasks before the Congress to repair the damage and enact a strong anti-inflation law.

As a part of our program to keep our country strong, we are determined to preserve the financial strength of the Government. This means high taxes over the next few years. We must see to it that these taxes are shared among the people as fairly as possible. I expect to discuss these matters in the Economic Report and the Budget Message which will soon be presented to the Congress.

Our tax laws must be fair. And we must make absolutely certain they are administered fairly, without fear or favor of any kind for anybody. To this end, steps have already been taken to remedy weaknesses which have been disclosed in the administration of the tax laws. In addition, I hope the Congress will approve my reorganization plan for the Bureau of Internal Revenue. We must do everything necessary in order to make just as certain as is humanly possible that every taxpayer receives equal treatment under the law.

To carry the burden of defense we must have a strong, productive, and expanding economy here at home. We cannot neglect those things that have made us the great and powerful nation we are today.

Our strength depends upon the health, the morale, the freedom of our people. We can take on the burden of leadership in the fight for world peace because, for nearly 20 years, the Government and the people have been working together for the general welfare. We have given more and more of out citizens a fair chance at decent, useful, productive lives. That is the reason we are as strong as we are today.

This Government of ours—the Congress and the executive both—must keep on working to bring about a fair deal for all the American people. Some people will say that we haven't the time or the money this year for measures for the welfare of the people. But if we want to win the fight for peace, this is a part of the job we cannot ignore.

We will have to give up some things, we will have to go forward on others at a slower pace. But, so far as I am concerned, I do not think we can give up the things that are vital to our national strength.

I believe most people in this country will agree with me on that.

I think most farmers understand that soil conservation and rural electrification and agricultural research are not frills or luxuries, but real necessities in order to boost our farm production.

I think most workers understand that decent housing and good working conditions are not luxuries, but necessities if the working men and women of this country are to continue to out-produce the rest of the world.

I think our businessmen know that scientific research and transportation services and more steel mills and power projects are not luxuries, but necessities to keep our business and our industry in the forefront of industrial progress.

I think everybody knows that social insurance and better schools and health services are not frills, but necessities in helping all Americans to be useful and productive citizens, who can contribute their full share in the national effort to protect and advance our way of life.

We cannot do all we want to in times like these—we have to choose the things that will contribute most to defense—but we must continue to make progress if we are to be a strong nation in the years ahead.

Let me give you some examples.

We are going right ahead with the urgently needed work to develop our natural resources, to conserve our soil, and to prevent floods. We are going to produce essential power and build the lines that are necessary and that we have to have to transmit it to our farms and factories. We are going to encourage exploration for new mineral deposits.

We are going to keep on building essential highways and taking any other steps that will assure the Nation an adequate transportation system—on land, on the sea, and in the air.

We must move right ahead this year to see that defense workers and soldiers' families get decent housing at rents they can afford to pay.

We must begin our long deferred program of Federal aid to education—to help the States meet the present crisis in the operation of our schools. And we must help with the construction of schools in areas where they are critically needed because of the defense effort.

We urgently need to train more doctors and other health personnel, through aid to medical education. We also urgently need to expand the basic public health services in our home communities—especially in defense areas. The Congress should go ahead with these two measures immediately.

I have set up an impartial commission to make a thorough study of the Nation's health needs. One of the things this commission is looking into is how to bring the cost of modern medical care within the reach of all the people. I have repeatedly recommended national health insurance as the best way to do this. So far as I know, it is still the best way. If there are any better answers, I hope this commission will find them. But of one thing I am sure: something must be done, and done soon.

This year we ought to make a number of urgently needed improvements in our social security law. For one thing, benefits under old-age and survivors insurance should be raised $5 a month above the present average of $42. For another thing, the States should be given special aid to help them increase public assistance payments. By doing these things now, we can ease the pressure of living costs for people who depend on those fixed payments.

We should also make some cost-of-living adjustments for those receiving veterans' compensation for death or disability incurred in the service of our country. In addition, now is the time to start a sensible program of readjustment benefits for our veterans who have seen service since the fighting broke out in Korea.

Another thing the Congress should do at this session is to strengthen our system of farm price supports to meet the defense emergency. The "sliding scale" in the price support law should not be allowed to penalize farmers for increasing production to meet defense needs. We should also find a new and less costly method for supporting perishable commodities than the law now provides.

We need to act promptly to improve our labor law. The Taft-Hartley Act has many serious and far-reaching defects. Experience has demonstrated this so clearly that even the sponsors of the act now admit that it needs to be changed. A fair law, fair to both management and labor, is indispensable to sound labor relations and to full, uninterrupted production. I intend to keep on working for a fair law until we get one.

As we build our strength to defend the freedom in the world, we ourselves must extend the benefits of freedom more widely among all our own people. We need to take action toward the wider enjoyment of civil rights. Freedom is the birthright of every American.

The executive branch has been making real progress toward full equality of treatment and opportunity—in the Armed Forces, in the civil service, and in private firms working for the Government. Further advances require action by Congress, and I hope that means will be provided to give the Members of the Senate and the House a chance to vote on them.

I am glad to hear that home rule for the District of Columbia will be the first item of business before the Senate. I hope that it, as well as statehood for Hawaii and Alaska, will be adopted promptly.

All these measures I have been talking about—measures to advance the well-being of our people—demonstrate to the world the forward movement of our free society.

This demonstration of the way free men govern themselves has a more powerful influence on the people of the world—on both sides of the Iron Curtain—than all the trick slogans and pie-in-the-sky promises of the Communists.

But our shortcomings, as well as our progress, are watched from abroad. And there is one shortcoming I want to speak about plainly.

Our kind of government above all others cannot tolerate dishonesty among public servants.

Some dishonest people worm themselves into almost every human organization. It is all the more shocking, however, when they make their way into a Government such as ours, which is based on the principle of justice for all. Such unworthy public servants must be weeded out. I intend to see to it that Federal employees who have been guilty of misconduct are punished for it. I also intend to see to it that the honest and hard-working great majority of our Federal employees are protected against partisan slander and malicious attack.

I have already made some recommendations to the Congress to help accomplish these purposes. I intend to submit further recommendations to this end. I will welcome the wholehearted cooperation of the Congress in this effort.

I also think that the Congress can do a great deal to

strengthen confidence in our institutions by applying rigorous standards of moral integrity to its own operations, and by finding an effective way to control campaign expenditures, and by protecting the rights of individuals in congressional investigations.

To meet the crisis which now hangs over the world, we need many different kinds of strength—military, economic, political, and moral. And of all these, I am convinced that moral strength is the most vital.

When you come right down to it, it is the courage and the character of our Nation—and of each one of us as individuals-that will really decide how well we meet this challenge.

We are engaged in a great undertaking at home and abroad—the greatest, in fact, that any nation has ever been privileged to embark upon. We are working night and day to bring peace to the world and to spread the democratic ideals of justice and self-government to all people. Our accomplishments are already remarkable. We ought to be full of pride in what we are doing, and full of confidence and hope in the outcome. No nation ever had greater resources, or greater energy, or nobler traditions to inspire it.

And yet, day in and day out, we see a long procession of timid and fearful men who wring their hands and cry out that we have lost the way, that we don't know what we are doing, that we are bound to fail. Some say we should give up the struggle for peace, and others say we should have a war and get it over with. That's a terrible statement. I had heard it made, but they want us to forget the great objective of preventing another world war—the objective for which our soldiers have been fighting in the hills of Korea.

If we are to be worthy of all that has been done for us by our soldiers in the field, we must be true to the ideals for which they are fighting. We must reject the counsels of defeat and despair. We must have the determination to complete the great work for which our men have laid down their lives.

In all we do, we should remember who we are and what we stand for. We are Americans. Our forefathers had far greater obstacles than we have, and much poorer chances of success. They did not lose heart, or turn aside from their goals. In the darkest of all winters in American history, at Valley Forge, George Washington said: "We must not, in so great a contest, expect to meet with nothing but sunshine." With that spirit they won their fight for freedom.

We must have that same faith and vision. In the great contest in which we are engaged today, we cannot expect to have fair weather all the way. But it is a contest just as important for this country and for all men, as the desperate struggle that George Washington fought through to victory.

Let us prove, again, that we are not merely sunshine patriots and summer soldiers. Let us go forward, trusting in the God of Peace, to win the goals we seek.

State of the Union Address Harry S. Truman

January 7, 1953

To the Congress of the United States:

I have the honor to report to the Congress on the state of the Union.

This is the eighth such report that, as President, I have been privileged to present to you and to the country. On previous occasions, it has been my custom to set forth proposals for legislative action in the coming year. But that is not my purpose today. The presentation of a legislative program falls properly to my successor, not to me, and I would not infringe upon his responsibility to chart the forward course. Instead, I wish to speak of the course we have been following the past eight years and the position at which we have arrived.

In just two weeks, General Eisenhower will be inaugurated as President of the United States and I will resume—most gladly—my 'place as a private citizen of this Republic. The Presidency last changed hands eight years ago this coming April. That was a tragic time: a time of grieving for

President Roosevelt—the great and gallant human being who had been taken from us; a time of unrelieved anxiety to his successor, thrust so suddenly into the complexities and burdens of the Presidential office.

Not so this time. This time we see the normal transition under our democratic system. One President, at the conclusion of his term, steps back to private life; his successor, chosen by the people, begins his tenure of the office. And the Presidency of the United States continues to function without a moment's break.

Since the election, I have done my best to assure that the transfer from one Administration to another shall be smooth and orderly. From General Eisenhower and his associates, I have had friendly and understanding collaboration in this endeavor. I have not sought to thrust upon him—nor has he sought to take—the responsibility which must be mine until twelve o'clock noon on January twentieth. But together, I hope and believe we have found means whereby the incoming President can obtain the full and detailed information he will need to assume the responsibility the moment he takes the oath of office.

The President-elect is about to take up the greatest burdens, the most compelling responsibilities, given to any man. And I, with you and all Americans, wish for him all possible success in undertaking the tasks that will so soon be his.

What are these tasks? The President is Chief of State, elected representative of all the people, national spokesman for them and to them. He is Commander-in-Chief of our armed forces. He is charged with the conduct of our foreign relations. He is Chief Executive of the Nation's largest civilian organization. He must select and nominate all top officials of the Executive Branch and all Federal judges.

And on the legislative side, he has the obligation and the opportunity to recommend, and to approve or veto legislation. Besides all this, it is to him that a great political party turns naturally for leadership, and that, too, he must provide as President.

This bundle of burdens is unique; there is nothing else like it on the face of the earth. Each task could be a full-time job. Together, they would be a tremendous undertaking in the easiest of times.

But our times are not easy; they are hard-as hard and complex, perhaps as any in our history. Now, the President not only has to carry on these tasks in such a way that our democracy may grow and flourish and our people prosper, but he also has to lead the whole free world in overcoming the communist menace—and all this under the shadow of the atomic bomb.

This is a huge challenge to the human being who occupies the Presidential office. But it is not a challenge to him alone, for in reality he cannot meet it alone. The challenge runs not just to him but to his whole Administration, to the Congress, to the country.

Ultimately, no President can master his responsibilities, save as his fellow citizens-indeed, the whole people—comprehend the challenge of our times and move, with him, to meet it.

It has been my privilege to hold the Presidential office for nearly eight years now, and much has been done in which I take great pride. But this is not personal pride. It is pride in the people, in the Nation. It is pride in our political system and our form of government—balky sometimes, mechanically deficient perhaps, in many ways—but enormously alive and vigorous; able through these years to keep the Republic on the right course, rising to the great occasions, accomplishing the essentials, meeting the basic challenge of our times.

There have been misunderstandings and controversies these past eight years, but through it all the President of the United States has had that measure of support and understanding without which no man could sustain the burdens of the Presidential office, or hope to discharge its responsibilities.

For this I am profoundly grateful—grateful to my associates in the Executive Branch—most of them non-partisan civil servants; grateful—despite our disagreements-to the Members of the Congress on both sides of the aisle; grateful especially to the American people, the citizens of this Republic, governors of us all.

We are still so close to recent controversies that some of us may find it hard to understand the accomplishments of these past eight years. But the accomplishments are real and very great, not as the President's, not as the Congress', but as the achievements of our country and all the people in it.

Let me remind you of some of the things we have done since I first assumed my duties as President of the United States.

I took the oath of office on April 12, 1945. In May of that same year, the Nazis surrendered. Then, in July, that great white flash of light, man-made at Alamogordo, heralded swift and final victory in World War II—and opened the doorway to the atomic age.

Consider some of the great questions that were posed for us by sudden, total victory in World War II. Consider also, how well we as a Nation have responded.

Would the American economy collapse, after the war? That was one question. Would there be another depression here—a repetition of 1921 or 1929? The free world feared and dreaded it. The communists hoped for it and built their policies upon that hope.

We answered that question—answered it with a resounding "no."

Our economy has grown tremendously. Free enterprise has flourished as never fore. Sixty-two million people are now gainfully employed, compared with 51 million seven years ago. Private businessmen and farmers have invested more than 200 billion dollars in new plant and equipment since the end of World War II. Prices have risen further than they should have done—but incomes, by and large, have risen even more, so that real living standards are now considerably higher than seven years ago. Aided by sound government policies, our expanding economy has shown the strength and flexibility for swift and almost painless reconversion from war to peace, in 1945 and 1946; for quick reaction and recovery— well before Korea—from the beginnings of recession in 1949. Above all, this live and vital economy of ours has now shown the remarkable capacity to sustain a great mobilization program for defense, a vast outpouring of aid to friends and allies all around the world—and still to produce more goods and services for peaceful use at home than we have ever known before.

This has been our answer, up to now, to those who feared or hoped for a depression in this country.

How have we handled our national finances? That was another question arising at war's end. In the administration of the Government, no problem takes more of the President's time, year in and year out, than fashioning the Budget, and the related problem of managing the public debt.

Financing World War II left us with a tremendous public debt, which reached 279 billion dollars at its peak in February, 1946.

Beginning in July, 1946, when war and reconversion financing had ended, we have held quite closely to the sound standard that in times of high employment and high national income, the Federal Budget should be balanced and the debt reduced.

For the four fiscal years from July 1, 1946, to June 30, 1950, we had a net surplus of 4.3 billion dollars. Using this surplus, and the Treasury's excess cash reserves, the debt was reduced substantially, reaching a low point of 251 billion dollars in June, 1949, and ending up at 257 billion dollars on June 30, 1950.

In July of 1950, we began our rapid rearmament, and for two years held very close to a pay-as-we-go policy. But in the current fiscal year and the next, rising expenditures for defense will substantially outrun receipts. This will pose an immediate and serious problem for the new Congress.

Now let me turn to another question we faced at the war's end. Would we take up again, and carry forward, the great projects of social welfare—so badly needed, so long overdue—that the New Deal had introduced into our national life? Would our Government continue to have a heart for the people, or was the progress of the New Deal to be halted in the aftermath of war as decisively as the progress of Woodrow Wilson's New Freedom had been halted after the first world war?

This question, too, we have answered. We have answered it by doubling old age insurance benefits and extending coverage to ten million more people. We have answered it by increasing our minimum wage. We have answered by the three million privately constructed homes that the Federal Government has helped finance since the war—and the 155 thousand units of low rent public housing placed under construction since 1949.

We have answered with the 42 thousand new hospital beds provided since 1946 through the joint efforts of the Federal Government and local communities.

We have answered by helping eight million veterans of World War II to obtain advanced education, 196 thousand to start in business, and 64 thousand to buy farms.

We have answered by continuing to help farmers obtain electric power, until today nearly 90 per cent of our farms have power line electric service.

In these and other ways, we have demonstrated, up to now, that our democracy has not forgotten how to use the powers of the Government to promote the people's welfare and security.

Another of the big post-war questions was this: What we would do with the Nation's natural resources—its soils and water, forests and grasslands. Would we continue the strong conservation movement of the 1930's, or would we, as we did after the First World War, slip back into the practices of monopoly, exploitation, and waste ?

The answer is plain. All across our country, the soil conservation movement has spread, aided by Government programs, enriching private and public lands, preserving them from destruction, improving them for future use. In our river basins, we have invested nearly 5 billion dollars of public funds in the last eight years—invested them in projects to control floods, irrigate farmlands, produce low-cost power and get it to the housewives and farmers and businessmen who need it. We have been vigilant in protecting the people's property—lands and forests and oil and minerals.

We have had to fight hard against those who would use our resources for private greed; we have met setbacks; we have had to delay work because of defense priorities, but on the whole we can be proud of our record in protecting our natural heritage, and in using our resources for the public good.

Here is another question we had to face at the war's close: Would we continue, in peace as well as war, to promote equality of opportunity for all our citizens, seeking ways and means to guarantee for all of them the full enjoyment of their civil rights?

During the war we achieved great economic and social gains for millions of our fellow citizens who had been held back by prejudice. Were we prepared, in peacetime, to keep on moving toward full realization of the democratic promise? Or would we let it be submerged, wiped out, in post-war riots and reaction, as after World War I?

We answered these questions in a series of forward steps at every level of government and in many spheres of private life. In our armed forces, our civil service, our universities, our railway trains, the residential districts of our cities—in stores and factories all across the Nation—in the polling booths as well—the barriers are coming down. This is happening, in part, at the mandate of the courts; in part, at the insistence of Federal, State and local governments; in part, through the enlightened action of private groups and persons in every region and every walk of life.

There has been a great awakening of the American conscience on the issues of civil rights. And all this progress—still far from complete but still continuing—has been our answer, up to now, to those who questioned our intention to live up to the promises of equal freedom for us all.

There was another question posed for us at the war's end, which equally concerned the future course of our democracy: Could the machinery of government and politics in this Republic be changed, improved, adapted rapidly enough to carry through, responsibly and well, the vast, new complicated undertakings called for in our time ?

We have answered this question, too, answered it by tackling the most urgent, most specific, problems which the war experience itself had brought into sharp focus. The reorganization of the Congress in 1946; the unification of our armed services, beginning in 1947; the closer integration of foreign and military policy through the National Security Council created that same year; and the Executive reorganizations, before and after the Hoover-Acheson Commission Report in 1949—these are landmarks in our continuing endeavor to make government an effective instrument of service to the people.

I come now to the most vital question of all, the greatest of our concerns: Could there be built in the world a durable structure of security, a lasting peace for all the nations, or would we drift, as after World War I, toward another terrible disaster—a disaster which this time might be the holocaust of atomic war ?

That is still the overriding question of our time. We cannot know the answer yet; perhaps we will not know it finally for a long time to come. But day and night, these past eight years, we have been building for peace, searching out the way that leads most surely to security and freedom and justice in the world for us and all mankind.

This, above all else, has been the task of our Republic since the end of World War II, and our accomplishment so far should give real pride to all Americans. At the very least, a total war has been averted, each day up to this hour. And at the most, we may already have succeeded in establishing conditions which can keep that kind of war from happening, for as far ahead as man can see.

The Second World War radically changed the power relationships of the world. Nations once great were left shattered and weak, channels of communication, routes of trade, political and economic ties of many kinds were ripped apart.

And in this changed, disrupted, chaotic situation, the United States and the Soviet Union emerged as the two strongest powers of the world. Each had tremendous human and natural resources, actual or potential, on a scale unmatched by any other nation.

Nothing could make plainer why the world is in its present state—and how that came to pass—than an understanding of the diametrically opposite principles and policies of these two great powers in a war-ruined world.

For our part, we in this Republic were-and are—free men, heirs of the American Revolution, dedicated to the truths of our Declaration of Independence:

"... That all men are created equal, that they are endowed by their Creator with certain unalienable rights... That to secure these rights, governments are instituted among men, deriving their just powers from the consent of the governed."

Our post-war objective has been in keeping with this great idea. The United States has sought to use its pre-eminent position of power to help other nations recover from the damage and dislocation of the war. We held out a helping hand to enable them to restore their national lives and to regain their positions as independent, self-supporting members of the great family of nations. This help was given without any attempt on our part to dominate or control any nation. We did not want satellites but partners.

The Soviet Union, however, took exactly the opposite course.

Its rulers saw in the weakened condition of the world not an obligation to assist in the great work of reconstruction, but an opportunity to exploit misery and suffering for the extension of their power. Instead of help, they brought subjugation. They extinguished, blotted out, the national independence of the countries that the military operations of World War II had left within their grasp.

The difference stares at us from the map of Europe today. To the west of the line that tragically divides Europe we see nations continuing to act and live in the light of their own traditions and principles. On the other side, we see the dead uniformity of a tyrannical system imposed by the rulers of the Soviet Union. Nothing could point up more clearly what the global struggle between the free world and the communists is all about.

It is a struggle as old as recorded history; it is freedom versus tyranny.

For the dominant idea of the Soviet regime is the terrible conception that men do not have rights but live at the mercy of the state.

Inevitably this idea of theirs—and all the consequences flowing from it—collided with the efforts of free nations to build a just and peaceful world. The "cold war" between the communists and the free world is nothing more or less than the Soviet attempt to checkmate and defeat our peaceful purposes, in furtherance of their own dread objective.

We did not seek this struggle, God forbid. We did our utmost to avoid it. In World War II, we and the Russians had fought side by side, each in our turn attacked and forced to combat by the aggressors. After the war, we hoped that our wartime collaboration could be maintained, that the frightful experience of Nazi invasion, of devastation in the heart of Russia, had turned the Soviet rulers away from their old proclaimed allegiance to world revolution and communist dominion. But instead, they violated, one by one, the solemn agreements they had made with us in wartime. They sought to use the rights and privileges they had obtained in the United Nations, to frustrate its purposes and cut down its powers as an effective agent of world progress and the keeper of the world's peace.

Despite this outcome, the efforts we made toward peaceful collaboration are a source of our present strength. They demonstrated that we believed what we proclaimed, that we actually sought honest agreements as the way to peace. Our whole moral position, our leadership in the free world today, is fortified by that fact.

The world is divided, not through our fault or failure, but by Soviet design. They, not we, began the cold war. And because the free world saw this happen because men know we made the effort and the Soviet rulers spurned it—the free nations have accepted leadership from our Republic, in meeting and mastering the Soviet offensive.

It seems to me especially important that all of us be clear, in our own thinking, about the nature of the threat we have faced-and will face for a long time to come. The measures we have devised to meet it take shape and pattern only as we understand what we were—and are—up against.

The Soviet Union occupies a territory of 8 million square miles. Beyond its borders, East and West, are the nearly five million square miles of the satellite states—virtually incorporated into the Soviet Union—and of China, now its close partner. This vast land mass contains an enormous store of natural resources sufficient to support an economic development comparable to our own.

That is the Stalinist world. It is a world of great natural diversity in geography and climate, in distribution of resources, in population, language, and living standards, in economic and cultural development. It is a world whose people are not all convinced communists by any means. It is a world where history and national traditions, particularly in its borderlands, tend more toward separation than unification, and run counter to the enforced combination that has been made of these areas today.

But it is also a world of great man-made uniformities, a world that bleeds its population white to build huge military forces; a world in which the police are everywhere and their authority unlimited; a world where terror and slavery are deliberately administered both as instruments of government and as means of production; a world where all effective social power is the state's monopoly—yet the state itself is the creature of the communist tyrants.

The Soviet Union, with its satellites, and China are held in the tight grip of communist party chieftains. The party dominates all social and political institutions. The party regulates and centrally directs the whole economy. In Moscow's sphere, and in Peiping's, all history, philosophy, morality and law are centrally established by rigid dogmas, incessantly drummed into the whole population and subject to interpretation—or to change by none except the party's own inner circle.

And lest their people learn too much of other ways of life, the communists have walled off their world, deliberately and uniformly, from the rest of human society.

That is the communist base of operation in their cold war. In addition, they have at their command hundreds and thousands of dedicated foreign communists, people in nearly every free country who will serve Moscow's ends. Thus the masters of the Kremlin are provided with deluded followers all through the free world whom they can manipulate, cynically and quite ruthlessly, to serve the purposes of the Soviet state.

Given their vast internal base of operations, and their agents in foreign lands, what are the communist rulers trying to do?

Inside their homeland, the communists are trying to maintain and modernize huge military forces. And simultaneously, they are endeavoring to weld their whole vast area and population into a completely self-contained, advanced industrial society. They aim, some day, to equal or better the production levels of Western Europe and North

America combined—thus shifting the balance of world economic power, and war potential, to their side.

They have a long way to go and they know it. But they are prepared to levy upon living generations any sacrifice that helps strengthen their armed power, or speed industrial development.

Externally, the communist rulers are trying to expand the boundaries of their world, whenever and wherever they can. This expansion they have pursued steadfastly since the close of World War II, using any means available to them.

Where the Soviet army was present, as in the countries of Eastern Europe, they have gradually squeezed free institutions to death.

Where post-war chaos existed in industrialized nations, as in Western Europe, the local Stalinists tried to gain power through political processes, politically-inspired strikes, and every available means for subverting free institutions to their evil ends.

Where conditions permitted, the Soviet rulers have stimulated and aided armed insurrection by communist-led revolutionary forces, as in Greece, Indo-China, the Philippines, and China, or outright aggression by one of their satellites, as in Korea.

Where the forces of nationalism, independence, and economic change were at work throughout the great sweep of Asia and Africa, the communists tried to identify themselves with the cause of progress, tried to picture themselves as the friends of freedom and advancement—surely one of the most cynical efforts of which history offers record.

Thus, everywhere in the free world, the communists seek to fish in troubled waters, to seize more countries, to enslave more millions of human souls. They were, and are, ready to ally themselves with any group, from the extreme left to the extreme right, that offers them an opportunity to advance their ends.

Geography gives them a central position. They are both a European and an Asian power, with borders touching many of the most sensitive and vital areas in the free world around them. So situated, they can use their armies and their economic power to set up simultaneously a whole series of threats—or inducements—to such widely dispersed places as Western Germany, Iran, and Japan. These pressures and attractions can be sustained at will, or quickly shifted from place to place.

Thus the communist rulers are moving, with implacable will, to create greater strength in their vast empire, and to create weakness and division in the free world, preparing for the time their false creed teaches them must come: the time when the whole world outside their sway will be so torn by strife and contradictions that it will be ripe for the communist plucking.

This is the heart of the distorted Marxist interpretation of history. This is the glass through which Moscow and Peiping look out upon the world, the glass through which they see the rest of us. They seem really to believe that history is on their side. And they are trying to boost "history" along, at every opportunity, in every way they can.

I have set forth here the nature of the communist menace confronting our Republic and the whole free world. This is the measure of the challenge we have faced since World War

II—a challenge partly military and partly economic, partly moral and partly intellectual, confronting us at every level of human endeavor and all around the world.

It has been and must be the free world's purpose not only to organize defenses against aggression and subversion, not only to build a structure of resistance and salvation for the community of nations outside the iron curtain, but in addition to give expression and opportunity to the forces of growth and 'progress in the free world, to so organize and unify the cooperative community of free men that we will not crumble but grow stronger over the years, and the Soviet empire, not the free world, will eventually have to change its ways or fall.

Our whole program of action to carry out this purpose has been directed to meet two requirements.

The first of these had to do with security. Like the pioneers who settled this great continent of ours, we have had to carry a musket while we went about our peaceful business. We realized that if we and our allies did not have military strength to meet the growing Soviet military threat, we would never have the opportunity to carry forward our efforts to build a peaceful world of law and order—the only environment in which our free institutions could survive and flourish.

Did this mean we had to drop everything else and concentrate on armies and weapons ? Of course it did not: side-by-side with this urgent military requirement, we had to continue to help create conditions of economic and social progress in the world. This work had to be carried forward alongside the first, not only in order to meet the non-military aspects of the communist drive for power, but also because this creative effort toward human progress is essential to bring about the kind of world we as free men want to live in.

These two requirements—military security and human progress—are more closely related in action than we sometimes recognize. Military security depends upon a strong economic underpinning and a stable and hopeful political order; conversely, the confidence that makes for economic and political progress does not thrive in areas that are vulnerable to military conquest.

These requirements are related in another way. Both of them depend upon unity of action among the free nations of the world. This, indeed, has been the foundation of our whole effort, for the drawing together of the free people of the world has become a condition essential not only to their progress, but to their survival as free people.

This is the conviction that underlies all the steps we have been taking to strengthen and unify the free nations during the past seven years.

What have these steps been? First of all, how have we gone about meeting the requirement of providing for our security against this world-wide challenge?

Our starting point, as I have said on many occasions, has been and remains the United Nations.

We were prepared, and so were the other nations of the free world, to place our reliance on the machinery of the United Nations to safeguard peace. But before the United Nations could give full expression to the concept of international security embodied in the Charter, it was essential that the five permanent members of the Security Council honor their solemn pledge to cooperate to that end. This the Soviet Union has not done.

I do not need to outline here the dreary record of Soviet obstruction and veto and the unceasing efforts of the Soviet representatives to sabotage the United Nations. It is important, however, to distinguish clearly between the principle of collective security embodied in the Charter and the mechanisms of the United Nations to give that principle effect. We must frankly recognize that the Soviet Union has been able, in certain instances, to stall the machinery of collective security. Yet it has not been able to impair the principle of collective security. The free nations of the world have retained their allegiance to that idea. They have found the means to act despite the Soviet veto, both through the United Nations itself and through the application of this principle in regional and other security arrangements that are fully in harmony with the Charter and give expression to its purposes.

The free world refused to resign itself to collective suicide merely because of the technicality of a Soviet veto.

The principle of collective measures to forestall aggression has found expression in the Treaty of Rio de Janeiro, the North Atlantic Treaty, now extended to include Greece and Turkey, and the several treaties we have concluded to reinforce security in the Pacific area.

But the free nations have not this time fallen prey to the dangerous illusion that treaties alone will stop an aggressor. By a series of vigorous actions, as varied as the nature of the threat, the free nations have successfully thwarted aggression or the threat of aggression in many different parts of the world.

Our country has led or supported these collective measures. The aid we have given to people determined to act in defense of their freedom has often spelled the difference between success and failure.

We all know what we have done, and I shall not review in detail the steps we have taken. Each major step was a milepost in the developing unity, strength and resolute will of the free nations.

The first was the determined and successful effort made through the United Nations to safeguard the integrity and independence of Iran in 1945 and 1946.

Next was our aid and support to embattled Greece, which enabled her to defeat the forces threatening her national independence.

In Turkey, cooperative action resulted in building up a bulwark of military strength for an area vital to the defenses of the entire free world.

In 1949, we began furnishing military aid to our partners in the North Atlantic Community and to a number of other free countries.

The Soviet Union's threats against Germany and Japan, its neighbors to the West and to the East, have been successfully withstood. Free Germany is on its way to becoming a member of the peaceful community of nations, and a partner in the common defense. The Soviet effort to capture Berlin by blockade was thwarted by the courageous Allied airlift. An independent and democratic Japan has been brought back into the community of free nations.

In the Far East, the tactics of communist imperialism have reached heights of violence unmatched elsewhere—and the problem of concerted action by the free nations has been at once more acute and more difficult.

Here, in spite of outside aid and support, the free government of China succumbed to the communist assault. Our aid has enabled the free Chinese to rebuild and strengthen their forces on the island of Formosa. In other areas of the Far East-in Indo-China, Malaya, and the Philippines—our assistance has helped sustain a staunch resistance against communist insurrectionary attacks.

The supreme test, up to this point, of the will and determination of the free nations came in Korea, when communist forces invaded the Republic of Korea, a state that was in a special sense under the protection of the United Nations. The response was immediate and resolute. Under our military leadership, the free nations for the first time took up arms, collectively, to repel aggression.

Aggression was repelled, driven back, punished. Since that time, communist strategy has seen fit to prolong the conflict, in spite of honest efforts by the United Nations to reach an honorable truce. The months of deadlock have demonstrated that the communists cannot achieve by persistence, or by diplomatic trickery, what they failed to achieve by sneak attack. Korea has demonstrated that the free world has the will and the endurance to match the communist effort to overthrow international order through local aggression.

It has been a bitter struggle and it has cost us much in brave lives and human suffering, but it has made it plain that the free nations will fight side by side, that they will not succumb to aggression or intimidation, one by one. This, in the final analysis, is the only way to halt the communist drive to world power.

At the heart of the free world's defense is the military

strength of the United States.

From 1945 to 1949, the United States was sole possessor of the atomic bomb. That was a great deterrent and protection in itself.

But when the Soviets produced an atomic explosion—as they were bound to do in time—we had to broaden the whole basis of our strength. We had to endeavor to keep our lead in atomic weapons. We had to strengthen our armed forces generally and to enlarge our productive capacity-our mobilization base. Historically, it was the Soviet atomic explosion in the fall of 1949, nine months before the aggression in Korea, which stimulated the planning for our program of defense mobilization.

What we needed was not just a central force that could strike back against aggression. We also needed strength along the outer edges of the free world, defenses for our allies as well as for ourselves, strength to hold the line against attack as well as to retaliate.

We have made great progress on this task of building strong defenses. In the last two and one half years, we have more than doubled our own defenses, and we have helped to increase the protection of nearly all the other free nations.

All the measures of collective security, resistance to aggression, and the building of defenses, constitute the first requirement for the survival and progress of the free world. But, as I have pointed out, they are interwoven with the necessity of taking steps to create and maintain economic and social progress in the free nations. There can be no military strength except where there is economic capacity to back it. There can be no freedom where there is economic chaos or social collapse. For these reasons, our national policy has included a wide range of economic measures.

In Europe, the grand design of the Marshall Plan permitted the people of Britain and France and Italy and a half dozen other countries, with help from the United States, to lift themselves from stagnation and find again the path of rising production, rising incomes, rising standards of living. The situation was changed almost overnight by the Marshall Plan; the people of Europe have a renewed hope and vitality, and they are able to carry a share of the military defense of the free world that would have been impossible a few years ago.

Now the countries of Europe are moving rapidly towards political and economic unity, changing the map of Europe in more hopeful ways than it has been changed for 500 years. Customs unions, European economic institutions like the Schuman Plan, the movement toward European political integration, the European Defense Community-all are signs of practical and effective growth toward greater common strength and unity. The countries of Western Europe, including the free Republic of Germany are working together, and the whole free world is the gainer.

It sometimes happens, in the course of history, that steps taken to meet an immediate necessity serve an ultimate purpose greater than may be apparent at the time. This, I believe, is the meaning of what has been going on in Europe under the threat of aggression. The free nations there, with our help, have been drawing together in defense of their free institutions. In so doing, they have laid the foundations of a unity that will endure as a major creative force beyond the exigencies of this period of history. We may, at this close range, be but dimly aware of the creative surge this movement represents, but I believe it to be of historic importance. I believe its benefits will survive long after communist tyranny is nothing but an unhappy memory.

In Asia and Africa, the economic and social problems are different but no less urgent. There hundreds of millions of people are in ferment, exploding into the twentieth century, thrusting toward equality and independence and improvement in the hard conditions of their lives.

Politically, economically, socially, things cannot and will not stay in their pre-war mold in Africa and Asia. Change must come—is coming—fast. Just in the years I have been President, 12 free nations, with more than 600 million people, have become independent: Burma, Indonesia, the Philippines, Korea, Israel, Libya, India, Pakistan and Ceylon, and the three Associated States of Indo-China, now members of the French Union. These names alone are testimony to the sweep of the great force which is changing the face of half the world.

Working out new relationships among the peoples of the free world would not be easy in the best of times. Even if there were no Communist drive for expansion, there would be hard and complex problems of transition from old social forms, old political arrangements, old economic institutions to the new ones our century demands—problems of guiding change into constructive channels, of helping new nations grow strong and stable. But now, with the Soviet rulers striving to exploit this ferment for their own purposes, the task has become harder and more urgent—terribly urgent.

In this situation, we see the meaning and the importance of the Point IV program, through which we can share our store of know-how and of capital to help these people develop their economies and reshape their societies. As we help Iranians to raise more grain, Indians to reduce the incidence of malaria, Liberians to educate their children better, we are at once helping to answer the desires of the people for advancement, and demonstrating the superiority of freedom over communism. There will be no quick solution for any of the difficulties of the new nations of Asia and Africa—but there may be no solution at all if we do not press forward with full energy to help these countries grow and flourish in freedom and in cooperation with the rest of the free world.

Our measures of economic policy have already had a tremendous effect on the course of events. Eight years ago, the Kremlin thought post-war collapse in Western Europe and Japan—with economic dislocation in America—might give them the signal to advance. We demonstrated they were wrong. Now they wait with hope that the economic recovery of the free world has set the stage for violent and disastrous rivalry among the economically developed nations, struggling for each other's markets and a greater share of trade. Here is another test that we shall have to meet and master in the years immediately ahead. And it will take great ingenuity and effort—and much time—before we prove the Kremlin wrong again. But we can do it. It is true that economic recovery presents its problems, as does economic decline, but they are problems of another order. They are the problems of distributing abundance fairly, and they can be solved by the process of international cooperation that has already brought us so far.

These are the measures we must continue. This is the path we must follow. We must go on, working with our free associates, building an international structure for military defense, and for economic, social, and political progress. We must be prepared for war, because war may be thrust upon us. But the stakes in our search for peace are immensely higher than they have ever been before.

For now we have entered the atomic age, and war has

undergone a technological change which makes it a very different thing from what it used to be. War today between the Soviet empire and the free nations might dig the grave not only of our Stalinist opponents, but of our own society, our world as well as theirs.

This transformation has been brought to pass in the seven years from Alamogordo to Eniwetok. It is only seven years, but the new force of atomic energy has turned the world into a very different kind of place.

Science and technology have worked so fast that war's new meaning may not yet be grasped by all the .peoples who would be its victims; nor, perhaps, by the rulers in the Kremlin. But I have been President of the United States, these seven years, responsible for the decisions which have brought our science and our engineering to their present place. I know what this development means now. I know something of what it will come to mean in the future.

We in this Government realized, even before the first successful atomic explosion, that this new force spelled terrible danger for all mankind unless it were brought under international control. We promptly advanced proposals in the United Nations to take this new source of energy out of the arena of national rivalries, to make it impossible to use it as a weapon of war. These proposals, so pregnant with benefit for all humanity, were rebuffed by the rulers of the Soviet Union.

The language of science is universal, the movement of science is always forward into the unknown. We could not assume that the Soviet Union would not develop the same weapon, regardless of all our precautions, nor that there were not other and even more terrible means of destruction lying in the unexplored field of atomic energy.

We had no alternative, then, but to press on, to probe the secrets of atomic power to the uttermost of our capacity, to maintain, if we could, our initial superiority in the atomic field. At the same time, we sought persistently for some avenue, some formula, for reaching an agreement with the Soviet rulers that would place this new form of power under effective restraints—that would guarantee no nation would use it in war. I do not have to recount here the proposals we made, the steps taken in the United Nations, striving at least to open a way to ultimate agreement. I hope and believe that we will continue to make these efforts so long as there is the slightest possibility of progress. All civilized nations are agreed on the urgency of the problem, and have shown their willingness to agree on effective measures of control—all save the Soviet Union and its satellites. But they have rejected every reasonable proposal.

Meanwhile, the progress of scientific experiment has outrun our expectations. Atomic science is in the full tide of development; the unfolding of the innermost secrets of matter is uninterrupted and irresistible. Since Alamogordo we have developed atomic weapons with many times the explosive force of the early models, and we have produced them in substantial quantities. And recently, in the thermonuclear tests at Eniwetok, we have entered another stage in the world-shaking development of atomic energy. From now on, man moves into a new era of destructive power, capable of creating explosions of a new order of magnitude, dwarfing the mushroom clouds of Hiroshima and Nagasaki.

We have no reason to think that the stage we have now reached in the release of atomic energy will be the last. Indeed, the speed of our scientific and technical progress over the last seven years shows no signs of abating. We are being hurried forward, in our mastery of the atom, from one discovery to another, toward yet unforeseeable peaks of destructive power.

Inevitably, until we can reach international agreement, this is the path we must follow. And we must realize that no advance we make is unattainable by others, that no advantage in this race can be more than temporary.

The war of the future would be one in which man could extinguish millions of lives at one blow, demolish the great cities of the world, wipe out the cultural achievements of the past—and destroy the very structure of a civilization that has been slowly and painfully built up through hundreds of generations.

Such a war is not a possible policy for rational men. We know this, but we dare not assume that others would not yield to the temptation science is now placing in their hands.

With that in mind, there is something I would say, to Stalin: You claim belief in Lenin's prophecy that one stage in the development of communist society would be war between your world and ours. But Lenin was a pre-atomic man, who viewed society and history with pre-atomic eyes. Something profound has happened since he wrote. War has changed its shape and its dimension. It cannot now be a "stage" in the development of anything save ruin for your regime and your homeland.

I do not know how much time may elapse before the communist rulers bring themselves to recognize this truth. But when they do, they will find us eager to reach understandings that will protect the world from the danger it faces today.

It is no wonder that some people wish that we had never succeeded in splitting the atom. But atomic power, like any other force of nature, is not evil in itself. Properly used, it is an instrumentality for human betterment. As a source of power, as a tool of scientific inquiry, it has untold possibilities. We are already making good progress in the constructive use of atomic power. We could do much more if we were free to concentrate on its peaceful uses exclusively.

Atomic power will be with us all the days of our lives. We cannot legislate it out of existence. We cannot ignore the dangers or the benefits it offers.

I believe that man can harness the forces of the atom to work for the improvement of the lot of human beings everywhere. That is our goal. As a nation, as a people, we must understand this problem, we must handle this new force wisely through our democratic processes. Above all, we must strive, in all earnestness and good faith, to bring it under effective international control. To do this will require much wisdom and patience and firmness. The awe-inspiring responsibility in this field now falls on a new Administration and a new Congress. I will give them my sup?port, as I am sure all our citizens will, in whatever constructive steps they may take to make this newest of man's discoveries a source of good and not of ultimate destruction.

We cannot tell when or whether the attitude of the Soviet rulers may change. We do not know how long it may be before they show a willingness to negotiate effective control of atomic energy and honorable settlements of other world problems. We cannot measure how deep-rooted are the Kremlin's illusions about us. We can be sure, however, that the rulers of the communist world will not change their basic objectives lightly or soon.

The communist rulers have a sense of time about these things wholly unlike our own. We tend to divide our future into short spans, like the two-year life of this Congress, or the four years of the next Presidential term. They seem to think and plan in terms of generations. And there is, therefore, no easy, short-run way to make them see that their plans cannot prevail.

This means there is ahead of us a long hard test of strength and stamina, between the free world and the communist domain-our politics and our economy, our science and technology against the best they can do—our liberty against their slavery—our voluntary concert Of free nations against their forced amalgam of "people's republics"—our strategy against their strategy-our nerve against their nerve.

Above all, this is a test of the will and the steadiness of the people of the United States.

There has been no challenge like this in the history of our Republic. We are called upon to rise to the occasion, as no people before us.

What is required of us is not easy. The way we must learn to live, the world we have to live in, cannot be so pleasant, safe or simple as most of us have known before, or confidently hoped to know.

Already we have had to sacrifice a number of accustomed ways of working and of living, much nervous energy, material resources, even human life. Yet if one thing is certain in our future, it is that more sacrifice still lies ahead.

Were we to grow discouraged now, were we to weaken and slack off, the whole structure we have built, these past eight years, would come apart and fall away. Never then, no matter by what stringent means, could our free world regain the ground, the time, the sheer momentum, lost by such a move. There can and should be changes and improvements in our programs, to meet new situations, serve new needs. But to desert the spirit of our basic policies, to step back from them now, would surely start the free world's slide toward the darkness that the communists have prophesied-toward the moment for which they watch and wait.

If we value our freedom and our way of life and want to see them safe, we must meet the challenge and accept its implications, stick to our guns and carry out our policies.

I have set out the basic conditions, as I see them, under which we have been working in the world, and the nature of our basic policies. What, then, of the future? The answer, I believe, is this: As we continue to confound Soviet expectations, as our world grows stronger, more united, more attractive to men on both sides of the iron curtain, then inevitably there will come a time of change within the communist world. We do not know how that change will come about, whether by deliberate decision in the Kremlin, by coup d'etat, by revolution, by defection of satellites, or perhaps by some unforeseen combination of factors such as these.

But if the communist rulers understand they cannot win by war, and if we frustrate their attempts to win by subversion, it is not too much to expect their world to change its character, moderate its aims, become more realistic and less implacable, and recede from the cold war they began.

Do not be deceived by the strong face, the look of monolithic power that the communist dictators wear before the outside world. Remember their power has no basis in consent. Remember they are so afraid of the free world's ideas and ways of life, they do not dare to let their people know about them. Think of the massive effort they put forth to try to stop our Campaign of Truth from reaching their people with its message of freedom.

The masters of the Kremlin live in fear their power and position would collapse were their own people to acquire knowledge, information, comprehension about our free society. Their world has many elements of strength, but this one fatal flaw: the weakness represented by their iron curtain and their police state. Surely, a social order at once so insecure and so fearful, must ultimately lose its competition with our free society.

Provided just one thing—and this I urge you to consider carefully—provided that the free world retains the confidence and the determination to outmatch the best our adversary can accomplish and to demonstrate for uncertain millions on both sides of the iron curtain the superiority of the free way of life.

That is the test upon all the free nations; upon none more than our own Republic.

Our resources are equal to the task. We have the industry, the skills, the basic economic strength. Above all, we have the vigor of free men in a free society. We have our liberties. And while we keep them, while we retain our democratic faith, the ultimate advantage in this hard competition lies with us, not with the communists.

But there are some things that could shift the advantage to their side. One of the things that could defeat us is fear—fear of the task we face, fear of adjusting to it, fear that breeds more fear, sapping our faith, corroding our liberties, turning citizen against citizen, ally against ally. Fear could snatch away the very values we are striving to defend.

Already the danger signals have gone up. Already the corrosive process bas begun. And every diminution of our tolerance, each new act of enforced conformity, each idle accusation, each demonstration of hysteria-each new restrictive law—is one more sign that we can lose the battle against fear.

The communists cannot deprive us of our liberties—fear can. The communists cannot stamp out our faith in human dignity-fear can. Fear is an enemy within ourselves, and if we do not root it out, it may destroy the very way of life we are so anxious to protect.

To beat back fear, we must hold fast to our heritage as free men. We must renew our confidence in one another, our tolerance, our sense of being neighbors, fellow citizens. We must take our stand on the Bill of Rights. The inquisition, the star chamber, have no place in a free society.

Our ultimate strength lies, not alone in arms, but in the sense of moral values and moral truths that give meaning and vitality to the purposes of free people. These values are our faith, our inspiration, the source of our strength and our indomitable determination.

We face hard tasks, great dangers. But we are Americans and we have faced hardships and uncertainty before, we have adjusted before to changing circumstances. Our whole history has been a steady training for the work it is now ours to do.

No one can lose heart for the task, none can lose faith in our free ways, who stops to remember where we began, what we have sought, and what accomplished, all together as Americans.

I have lived a long time and seen much happen in our country. And I know out of my own experience, that we can do what must be done.

When I think back to the country I grew up in—and then look at what our country has become—I am quite certain that having done so much, we can do more.

After all, it has been scarcely fifteen years since most Americans rejected out-of-hand the wise counsel that aggressors must be "quarantined". The very concept of collective security, the foundation-stone of all our actions now, was then strange doctrine, shunned and set aside. Talk about adapting; talk about adjusting; talk about responding as a people to the challenge of changed times and circumstances—there has never been a more spectacular example than this great change in America's outlook on the world.

Let all of us pause now, think back, consider carefully the meaning of our national experience. Let us draw comfort from it and faith, and confidence in our future as Americans.

The Nation's business is never finished. The basic questions we have been dealing with, these eight years past, present themselves anew. That is the way of our society. Circumstances change and current questions take on different forms, new complications, year by year. But underneath, the great issues remain the same—prosperity, welfare, human rights, effective democracy, and above all, peace.

Now we turn to the inaugural of our new President. And in the great work he is called upon to do he will have need for the support of a united people, a confident people, with firm faith in one another and in our common cause. I pledge him my support as a citizen of our Republic, and I ask you to give him yours.

To him, to you, to all my fellow citizens, I say, Godspeed.

May God bless our country and our cause.

www.ingramcontent.com/pod-product-compliance
Lightning Source LLC
Chambersburg PA
CBHW070635290526
45790CB00001B/103